Arthur Moffatt Lang at the age of 20

LAHORE TO LUCKNOW

Lahore to Lucknow

THE INDIAN MUTINY JOURNAL
OF ARTHUR MOFFATT LANG

Edited by
David Blomfield

Illustrations by
Julian Mann

Introduction by
Christopher Hibbert

LEO COOPER
LONDON

David Blomfield thanks innumerable members of his own family, the staff of the National Army Museum, the Royal Engineers Library, and the British Library's India Office Library and Department of Manuscripts, for the very considerable help he received during his research for this book.

First published in Great Britain in 1992 by
LEO COOPER
190 Shaftesbury Avenue, London WC2H 8JL
an imprint of
Pen & Sword Books Ltd.,
47 Church Street, Barnsley, South Yorkshire S70 2AS

A CIP catalogue record for this book is available
from the British Library

ISBN 0 85052 203 X

Typeset by Yorkshire Web, Barnsley, South Yorkshire
in Garamond Book 10 point

Printed in Great Britain by
Redwood Press
Melksham, Wiltshire

CONTENTS

ILLUSTRATIONS

MAPS

INTRODUCTION

by Christopher Hibbert
(Author of *The Great Mutiny India 1857*)

'This is splendid, no nonsense about it. We are fighting close up now, hurrying on the most rapid of sieges, working recklessly under fire.'

These words were written on the ridge outside Delhi on 12 September, 1857, and rarely has a young officer's intense excitement in the danger of war been so well conveyed.

On the evening of the next day their author, Lieutenant Arthur Moffatt Lang of the Bengal Engineers, was ordered to inspect the breach which the British Army's heavy guns had made in the walls surrounding the city. Behind these walls thousands of mutinous Indian troops were defying their British masters in the name of Bahadur Shah II, descendant of the Moghul Emperors who had ruled here before the British came. On the outcome of the proposed assault depended the immediate future of Britain's Empire in India.

Lieutenant Lang was told to climb up the steep slope towards the breach as soon as it was dark and to report as to whether or not an immediate assault was practicable. 'I preferred going when I could see,' his account continues, 'so went at once... and taking four riflemen crossed the road leading to the river... and slunk up through some trees to the foot of the glacis. Leaving my riflemen under a tree, I ran up the glacis and sat on the edge of the counterscarp and examined the appearance.... I ran back, fired at, and coming in was fired at by our own sentries.' In this characteristically modest way Lang described a brave reconnaissance which many thought should have won him a Victoria Cross. His concise report led to the British commanders deciding upon the assault on Delhi which was ordered to take place that night.

The letters and diaries in which Lang vividly describes this assault have long been known to historians of the Indian Mutiny. But they have not before been published in book form; and readers will be deeply grateful to Leo Cooper for bringing them out in this edition and to David Blomfield for his skilful editing.

Arthur Moffatt Lang's account is memorable both as a revealing self-portrait of a young Victorian officer and as a chronicle of the savage conflict in which he played so courageous a part. His delight in the excitement of war is evident from the moment he leaves Lahore for Delhi, choking with indignation, as he puts it, at the cruelty with which the poor ladies had been treated at Meerut, where the Mutiny had broken out, and hoping 'no quarter, no mercy will be the cry when we have the upper hand.'

It is extraordinary that Lang was not shot himself, that while taking part in some of the heaviest fighting of those years, he was not once hit until − when the conflict was almost over − he was sent spinning by a stinging crack on the shoulder from a bullet which glanced off his pouch-belt. At Agra he described riding through sepoys like a wild Crusader, 'slashing and thrusting'. At Delhi, where he scrambles breathlessly across the tumbled masonry, the bullets seem to pass like a hissing sheet of lead over his head. 'But on we rushed, shouting and cheering, while the grape and musketry from every street and from rampart and housetop knocked down men and officers. It was exciting to madness.'

As well as the sound of fury of fighting, Lang's diary evokes the beauty of the Indian landscape, the broad rivers with their green banks, the splendid, gleaming mosques and the red walls of forts glowing in the evening sunlight, forest walks where peacocks strut proudly beneath the trees and monkeys scamper and chatter in the branches, and over all is the strong scent of the babul blossoms. There are well-observed and entertaining character sketches: not least that of the Commander-in-Chief, Sir Colin Campbell himself, a Glaswegian carpenter's son with a ferocious temper and a sharp, pink, lively face, gesticulating with both hands and hissing through clenched teeth as he argues furiously with the Chief Engineer. There are glimpses, too, of English ladies in bonnets, cheering the troops as they march across the bridge into Agra; of picnics at the Taj Mahal and dances on its smooth marble floor. Contrasting with these is the pervading brutality, the horror of the scenes at Cawnpore where evidence of the massacre lies scattered upon every side – bloodstained slippers and socks and bits of clothing, letters and leaves of books and locks of long hair. 'No officer standing in these rooms spoke to another. I know I could not have spoken. I felt as if my heart was stone and my brain fire, and that the spot was enough to drive one mad.... I thought when I had killed twelve men outright at the battle of Agra, that I had done enough: I think now I shall never stop if I get a chance again.'

For all his protestations of hatred for the mutineers and for all the harsh treatment to which his own native soldiers were occasionally submitted at his hands, Lang was capable of profoundly tender feelings. He writes in moving terms of the death of his friend Home, a 'horrid dream' from which he 'longed to wake', and of that of Elliot Brownlow, 'such a splendid fellow, God bless him'. Indeed, the death of Brownlow 'cast a gloom over the campaign as far as it concerns me', he writes, 'and has rendered it distasteful to me and spoiled all my pleasure in war and victory and Lucknow'. The young man who had professed himself intensely happy while campaigning, who had thanked God that he had chosen to live the life of a soldier, now had had enough. He had been fighting as an infantry man, revelling in the excitement. He now wanted nothing more than to return to Lahore and to marry the girl with whom he had fallen in love before he left. So, declining more adventurous appointments, he went back to a comparatively humdrum life in Public Works.

His subsequent career was one of only moderate distinction. He was eventually promoted colonel and in 1908 awarded a C.B. It seemed a modest crowning honour for a soldier who had been recommended three times for the Victoria Cross and was four times mentioned in despatches. But he now at last has a fitting memorial: it is contained in the pages that follow.

By Lieutenant-General Sir Derek Lang KCB, DSO, MC

Is there room for another book on the Indian Mutiny? I believe there is when the material in it is taken direct from the diaries and journals of an eye witness, and Arthur Moffatt Lang (always referred to in our family as AML) was in the thick of the fighting at Delhi and Lucknow. This edition has been put together by David Blomfield, one of AML's grandsons by his second marriage. I am also a grandson − the son of AML's youngest son by his first marriage.

Despite the care with which the diaries and journals were written and with which his family preserved them, our grandfather never thought of publishing his own story of the Mutiny. He was too modest. He realized that, even among his family, not everyone would study the journals he sent home as carefully as his mother would. There is a nice touch in a letter to his brother George where he suggests that George was no doubt *told* to read them by an insistent parent!

Some of AML's colleagues, however, rushed into print. Medley, his 'companion of the breach', was one of the first. Medley's descriptions of the inspection of the breach (omitting AML's earlier inspection) and of the capture of Kadam Rasul were then used by all nineteenth-century historians, who naturally gave AML only minor billing. He made no effort to correct the story.

It was not until Field-Marshal Lord Roberts's autobiography was published in 1897, followed by the biography of Sir Alex Taylor by his daughter in 1913, that AML's role was recognised. AML let Taylor's daughter use his diary, and even added an 'explanation' for his bravery − his short-sightedness.

After AML's death, the diaries and journals remained in the family. Then, in 1930 the Society for Army Historical Research asked if they might publish excerpts. The editors, first Lieutenant-Colonel Leslie and then Colonel Molesworth, produced an admirably annotated series of selections for their military readership. There was, however, very little about AML as a family man. Quite naturally they concentrated on the military details.

In this edition, which is based primarily on the journal, there has been room for far more material. We can now see something of the man himself, of the family that formed so many of his ideals, of the romance of his proposal in the middle of the Mutiny year, of how it felt to witness what must have appeared to be the total dismemberment of British achievements and ideals.

He was a man, naturally gentle and forbearing, who showed deep respect for the 'Ladies', loved home, enjoyed sport, and displayed fervour for his religion. For the mutineers, however, he had a bitter hatred, and the Cawnpore massacre of women and children accentuated that hatred. Still, war in the mid-nineteenth century was hard and cruel; no quarter was given on either side, and the mutineers were as formidable opponents as any the British had encountered in their history. For his own part, AML too was proud of his profession of arms and was exhilarated by the excitement of combat. (Indeed his battle exploits would make thrilling cinema or television and are much healthier than the vandalistic violence on our screens today.) Once peace was restored, however, AML reverted to type and dedicated his working life to India's welfare.

There is still, however, much in his diaries that could not be included here. This book attempts to do no more than tell his story, and this alone involves a cast list of over 160. It includes every one of AML's close friends and those colleagues and commanders who played a major role in his life and the Mutiny. It keeps his comments on them and their actions. What it omits are his many very detailed lists of the actions, lives and – most especially – the deaths of many more officers and men, most of whom he scarcely knew. There is, therefore, still much more for historians to study, and many discoveries yet to be made.

In the 1930s the journal, diary and other AML letters of the Mutiny years were lodged in the British Library, where they were beautifully bound and preserved for future research. All major works on the Mutiny now include them in their bibliographies. A few quote from them, but only from those selections made by the Journal of the Society for Army Historical Research. Very few have consulted the diary or the journal. We hope that more will do so in the future.

An inevitable problem for any historian is that spelling does not stay the same. This is true of every country. Of India it is true as it is of nowhere else. In 1857 the effort to transcribe Indian words into English produced a situation where AML, who was anything but a careless writer, was within the year writing at one time 'Delhi' and at another 'Dehli'. So too he has Cabul and Cashmere where later in his own life he would be writing Kabul and Kashmir. (Oddly, 'Kashmere' is now the usual spelling of the Gate and Bastion he stormed in 1857 – close to his own spelling of 'Cashmere'.) The spelling of the places he knew then is now of course the concern of the people of India, Pakistan and Afghanistan. This edition therefore follows current usage, only using older forms (Cawnpore, Ganges, Jumna, Alam Bagh) where these are still acceptable alternatives. As AML was clearly quite happy to change his spellings to accord with current usage, who are we to do otherwise?

To help his readers interpret his journal AML would sometimes add maps. These sketches, slotted into the body of the text, were remarkably accurate, as might be expected of the man who was to draw the official map of the capture of Lucknow. The maps in this book are nearly all based on those sketch maps. Julian Mann has copied them line for line. Only the wording has been changed.

Julian Mann's illustrations too are either copied from contemporary photographs or from sketches made at the time by one of AML's fellow Bengal Engineers, Captain G. F. Atkinson, for the *Illustrated London News*. Atkinson did not serve at Delhi himself, but he was able to sketch the soldiers from life, along with their weapons and beasts of burden. It seems that he gathered the rest of his material from his fellow officers. It is therefore hardly surprising that there is an uncanny resemblance between AML and some of the figures in his drawings.

I first visited Delhi in 1957, a hundred years after the Mutiny, as a member of a group from the Canadian National Defence College. To my surprise I found that the Kashmere Gate — no longer of any significance and still in bad disrepair — had a memorial tablet leaning against it recording the siege in 1857. Later at a sumptuous dinner in Peshawar with the Pakistan Brigade, surrounded by magnificent silver memorabilia of the British Raj, three of us — the Pakistani Brigade Commander, a Canadian Brigadier, and I — were in conversation. After a while I noticed that the Canadian was no longer contributing to the discussion.

'John,' I said, 'what has happened? You are no longer with us!'

He laughed and said, 'I am the odd one out. You two share a much older tradition militarily than you share with us in Canada.'

He was of course quite right, and I believe many Indians and Pakistanis, civil and military, are grateful for the legacy left them by the Victorian British. We too, their British successors, should be equally grateful to AML and his generation for the help they gave in moulding those traditions, and for the subsequent privilege we enjoyed of fighting alongside the Indian Army in two world wars. Certainly my own memories of serving in the desert in World War Two with those magnificent warriors in their Fourth Division will never grow dim.

INDIA, 1857

14

CHAPTER 1

The Man and the Mutiny

THE MAN

'If ever I become a great hero, a second Iron Duke, what valuable documents will these sheets be for compiling the materials for a history of the early portion of this illustrious man's career!' In August, 1854, when he wrote these words to his mother in his customary neat black handwriting, 2nd-Lieutenant Arthur Moffatt Lang of the Bengal Engineers was in fact feeling anything but heroic. He had just arrived in Calcutta, was waiting to be sent to his first posting in the service of the East India Company and was finding Calcutta exceedingly dull. 'One must always be *en grande tenue*, always when out with a great black hat on, always with a dark coat and so on. It is as bad as London in its strict stiffness — in fact worse because everyone is so much better known. I find my short-sightedness a great enemy on the "course" for I shall get the credit of cutting everyone there soon. I hardly see one in ten in time to bow to them.'

Young Lang was never destined to become a great hero, nor indeed did he ever show the slightest wish to be one — he simply enjoyed spicing his letters home with elaborate self-mockery. However, fate almost took him at his word, and for just one year of his life he was to play a memorably heroic, if minor, role in one of the most bitter and bloody campaigns of the British Raj, and Lang's most famous act of heroism in that year he would ruefully ascribe to that same short-sightedness he so deplored on the course at Calcutta.

At the age of twenty-one Lang was certainly not looking for military glory. He had very different plans. He had passed out 'top of his batch' at the East India Company's Officer Training Seminary at Addiscombe, and as such was a holder of its coveted Pollock Medal. He was also an enthusiastic sportsman who had captained both the cricket and football teams. Yet he nursed no great ambitions to use his academic and physical talents as a fighting soldier. Like most of his contemporaries, he coveted an appointment either in the Company's Political Department as an administrator or as an Executive Engineer in its Public Works Department — and in 1854, he knew, the Company was in even greater need than usual for both administrators and engineers.

At that time the East India Company, generally referred to either as EIC or John Company, ruled virtually the whole of the sub-continent of India in the interests, and with the support, of the government of Great Britain. Under its Governor-General, with his headquarters in Calcutta, India was divided into three great Presidencies: Bombay, Madras and Bengal. In addition to these over the last few years, the Governor-General, Lord Dalhousie, had annexed, for what he saw as the most philanthropic reasons, both the Punjab and Oudh. Both had indeed been appallingly misgoverned in the past, but he was well aware that not all the inhabitants of these two new provinces would see philanthropy in quite the terms he did. He therefore decided to convince them of the benefits of Company rule by ensuring that they had the very best of administrators and engineers.

Although even then there was a large and well-trained Indian Civil Service, several of the Company's senior political officers and most of its civil engineers came from the ranks of the army. Able men were used wherever the Company needed them, regardless of their previous training or experience. Most officers welcomed the chance of such postings, as the pay and prospects for promotion were better there than in regimental service. Certainly Lang would welcome any such opportunity.

He had chosen his career with care and with real knowledge of what it involved. He came from a family whose roots were in India, and his parents were quite prepared, indeed eager, to see their children follow a way of life that would commit them to spending all their professional careers in one continent followed by retirement to another with which they had no more than certain distant, though very well maintained, family connections. It was after all what they had done themselves.

Lang's father had served in the Indian Civil Service as a respected judge in the North-West Provinces, and had recently retired to Harrow where he cut an equally respected, if engagingly eccentric, figure in literary society. Lang's grandfather, Robert Lang of Moor Park, had been a great bibliophile, the friend of Walter Scott and

SARAH LANG (1812-1880)

Lang's mother, to whom he addressed his journals, had nine children. None of her letters has survived, but his letters suggest that, very much the matriarch, she had spotted a wife for him back in England, if only he would wait for his first leave — ten years hence. In the event, however, he married — as she had done — within the Raj. Sarah's father, Lieutenant-General Richard Tickell, was also a Bengal Engineer. He could have been in Lang's mind at Delhi, for he too made his name by a daring single-handed inspection of a breach: it led to the capture of Gurrah Mandela in 1819. Like grandfather, like grandson.

owner of one of the finest private libraries in the land. Lang's mother, to whom he addressed his journals, was by birth a Tickell, a family descended from the minor eighteenth-century poet Thomas Tickell, but more recently known for the number of soldiers and administrators it contributed to the government of India.

Although he knew just what his chosen career entailed, Lang had spent hardly any time in India himself. Indeed he hardly knew his parents. Like most children of what were then described as 'Anglo-Indian' families, he had been sent home at the age of six to England for his education, and had been brought up by his aunt, Miss Mary Lang of Sudbury House, Harrow. Briefly, after his father's retirement and while he was himself being trained at Addiscombe, he and his parents were in the same country. Now they were once again divided by half the world, and were unlikely ever to meet again apart from the odd month or two of his home leave, which he could expect to be granted only once during his years of service.

He was, however, used to speaking to them through letters, and like most of his friends he would devote a remarkable amount of time to writing to them. To his mother he would send every few weeks his 'journal', some ten sheets of closely written, fluent prose, with scarcely a single correction, detailing what he had been doing, whom he had met and what he hoped to achieve. The journal was based very largely on his diary. This diary he wrote up every day of his adult life regardless of where he was. He would begin with a comment on the weather and then take the events of the day in the order they occurred. (On the last day of his life, when he was too weak to write it himself, the diary was filled in by his wife. That final entry gives the details of his last hours. It begins, however, with a description of the weather. He would have approved.)

The journal Lang sent home was less austere than the diary. It added lively descriptions of scenery and people, background information that would be essential to those at home. It was also less technical and occasionally less frank. He did not, for instance, copy from the diary for the 'dear home circle' the gorier or more technical details of the military actions in which he was involved, nor in rather different circumstances quite how many times he danced with this or that girl!

His journals (and the diaries) were carefully preserved by the family, and so too were many of his other letters, for he also wrote letters regularly to all his relations, many of whom kept them. To his father he would send just the occasional separate missive, often covering the more technical or more violent subjects, or referring specifically to meetings with his father's friends. To his sister Mary, (Pussy) — to whom he was very close — and to his brothers, the letters would be jocular (though occasionally, as in those to his third brother, the idle scamp Monty, the tone could be mock avuncular). He was very much the respected, beloved eldest brother, deeply concerned over his family's plans, partly perhaps because he found his father too vague and easy-going. Most especially, though not as often as he felt he should, he wrote to his Aunt Mary.

Mary Lang, his 'Englische Mutter' as he called her, had played a role typical of maiden aunts in Anglo-Indian middle-class families throughout the nineteenth and well into the twentieth century. She had enough money to maintain a large house in Harrow, and this was home to all her nephews throughout their schooldays (The younger brothers went to Harrow School, unlike Arthur who went first to Rugby and then to Cheltenham). Her house also provided a base for the few holidays his parents spent 'at home'. It was hardly surprising that on their retirement they too settled in Harrow.

Mary Lang probably deserves the credit for inculcating in her eldest nephew a real interest in art, architecture and literature. He had had a conventional public school education, which we can assume was very like that described in *Tom Brown's Schooldays*, as he specifically comments in his journal that he had been lent a copy and 'very much enjoyed reading it — so very truthful a picture of old Rugby life it is'. He clearly had a proper grounding in the classics and a scientific education appropriate to his career as an engineer, but he also had an interest in the arts, in botany and in entomology far beyond the conventional needs of his calling. When he eventually got away from the stifling conventions of Calcutta, his enthusiastic descriptions of the countryside and of the architecture of India were not simply those of a man who had in a sense come home. They were full of parallels drawn from the world of cultured Victorian society. He knew of, even if he had not visited, the great buildings and galleries of continental Europe. He was interested in the countryside not just as a landscape but as a subject for botanical study. For a conventional English gentleman — and he was most certainly that — he had had an unusually well-rounded education.

There was, however, one part of that education that clearly marked him more than any other. It was particularly important to him, to his family, and most certainly to his Aunt Mary. This was his religion. He was a devoted, extremely conscientious, unquestionably sincere, member of the Church of England.

Lang's religious convictions played a major role in everything he did and thought and planned over his first few years in India up to the outbreak of the Mutiny. They would do the same for the rest of his life. What happened to his religion in the stress of war was a different matter, a matter that obviously puzzled and distressed him. He often agonized over it in his diaries and letters, but clearly found no satisfactory answer.

In the early 1850s there was nothing especially unusual in a young officer in India holding very strong religious convictions. Young Lang was in good company. Since the days of the Lord Protector there had never been a time or a place where there were so many British officers who were committed Christians as there were in India in the 1850s. The major difference was that in India those officers, or at least those in political and administrative posts, were not only committed Christians; they were also extraordinarily competent at their jobs. Cromwell would have been amazed and overjoyed to have had just one or two men of comparable virtue and ability. In India their name was legion. They were the glory of the British Raj, yet ironically those same virtues and abilities were largely responsible for almost bringing the Raj down around their distinguished ears.

THE MUTINY

As every schoolchild is supposed to know, the Indian Mutiny was sparked off by the issue to the Indian Army of new cartridges that the Hindus thought were greased with cow fat and the Moslems thought were greased with pig. These cartridges, however, were not the *cause* of the Mutiny. Its cause lay far deeper than the issue of some new cartridges.

The Indian Army had been created in the eighteenth century by the EIC to defend the trade the Company had established and the property it had acquired. It was in many ways a most unusual institution. It was quite separate, and very different, from the British Army, which had several regiments of its own stationed in India. The British Army had British officers, British NCOs, and British troops. In the Indian Army, on the other hand, although each regiment was commanded by British officers (the Indian officers, however experienced they might be, played only subordinate roles) almost all the NCOs and all the troops were Indian (Exceptions to this were certain 'European' regiments and some of the artillery.).

At first this racial division in the Indian Army seemed to both nations both reasonable and efficient. The British had the money, the military expertise and the will to win. The Indians were used to mercenary service in armies of occupation, were enthusiastic soldiers and enjoyed the status given by employment in what was a smart and effective force. The Army flourished.

In the eighteenth century the British officers of the Indian Army still had something about them of the buccaneer. They may have had less professional training than officers in the British Army, but they had the dash their job required, and they knew their sepoys [troops] personally in a way that would have been unthinkable in most British regiments. They would even participate quite cheerfully alongside their troops in the occasional native festival, whether Hindu or Moslem. After all, their own religion was scarcely skin deep, if indeed professed at all. The relationship was, of course, never one of equals — it was properly paternalistic — but it was one that ensured that the troops respected their officers and that the officers recognized the men.

It was with the new century that something began to change. First, a new professionalism crept into the officer corps. This in itself was no bad thing. Indeed it began to attract to the Indian Army men of outstanding ability. The problem was that the more able the officer the more likely it was that he would be appointed to a political or executive post. The best officers were therefore no longer serving with the regiments. The less able ones were left to train the Army.

A further problem was that the officers of the native regiments were not only short on skills, they were short on numbers. When Lang himself was later to come face to face with the threat of major mutiny, it was from four native regiments in which the highest ranked officer on parade was a captain. Lang's own regiment was hardly better off. In 1846, for instance, twelve of the officers in the Bengal Engineers had civil administrative posts and twenty-six more were in the Public Works Department. Consequently at their headquarters at Roorkee the Bengal Sappers and Miners were officered by one major, one captain, and fourteen 2nd-lieutenants (several of whom had been transferred from infantry regiments and had no engineering training at all). When there was a war to be fought — and there recently had been major ones against the Afghans and against the Sikhs in the Punjab — the more senior officers had to abandon their roads and railways and resume their military careers, commanding troops about whom they knew nothing and in some cases cared even less.

It could of course be argued that the better qualified officers were doing even more important jobs as administrators. So they were, at least from the point of view of the civilian population. The administration of justice, the organization of services, the building of railways, roads and towns could hardly have been placed in better hands. It could even be argued that, at least in Bengal and the Punjab, when the Mutiny did break out it was virtually confined to the Indian Army only because the civilian population felt that they were better off with the British in control. However, it would be wrong simply to blame the weakness of the regimental officers for the Mutiny. It was just as much the fault of the good and the great who had left them in charge and gone off to run the country. The problem was that they were running the country almost too well for its own good; for in addition to the admirable changes they were making in the administration of justice, health and the economy, they were setting in train social changes for which the Indians were totally unprepared.

These social changes in India stemmed from changes in Britain itself, changes that had a profound effect on the moral character and convictions of the men who now came out to be officers in India. In the eighteenth century the officers had had very few convictions and even fewer conventional morals. They were mostly freebooters out for what they could get in the way of plunder. The Indians could understand that. What was the point of war if not for plunder? They could also sympathize with the officers taking Indian mistresses. After all the mistresses could teach the officers something of the Indian way of life. In the nineteenth century, however, a new breed of officer arrived with which they could not sympathize. These officers were men with morals, convictions, and perhaps even more significantly with wives — and those morals, convictions and wives were Christian.

These men were the first of what would later be called Victorians, many of them making their mark decades before the queen who gave her name to the century had been thought of, let alone sat on the throne. They were the true heirs of the evangelical movement of John Wesley. Though few of them would profess any commitment to Methodism, they shared the same commitment to Christianity. For the Indians this would be both a revelation and a threat.

Previously the British had interfered very little with Indian customs, however uncivilized they might appear. Now they set out to reform them. No longer would widows be allowed to throw themselves on their husbands' funeral pyres – this 'suttee' was wrong, according to the Christian creed. No longer could childless Rajahs adopt sons to whom to leave their kingdoms – such kingdoms had to be ceded to the British. No longer could Brahmin sepoys insist that they serve only in India – they must accept service overseas, even though they would lose caste because of it.

To the Indians in general, and to the sepoys in particular, it suddenly seemed that no one cared about the all-important matter of caste, nor indeed about the special requirements of Islam. Their British officers of the eighteenth century had understood them, but their officers now were either old and tired or young and inexperienced, while these political officers were rushing ahead with reforms that apparently were designed to destroy their beliefs.

The sepoys had never worried overmuch about nationalism. For them national pride was a luxury that only the rich could afford. Their religion, however, was quite another matter. Many of them were Brahmins, men of the highest caste, and their work as soldiers gave them added status. Now, however, it seemed that the British were for the first time eager to destroy that tradition and force them all into Christianity.

The sepoys were quite right in their instinctive fear of what this new generation of administrators was about. There was indeed a move to establish a more Christian way of life. Where they were wrong, however, was in the assumption that the social changes were part of a plot to convert them to Christianity. Despite their own convictions, very few of the British intended anything of the sort. However, there is no doubt that the sepoys feared that Christianity would be forced on them.

As a result, for the first six decades of the nineteenth century unrest in the Indian Army became almost endemic. It could, of course, be dealt with far more ruthlessly than would ever be allowed in the British Army, which was not in the habit of strapping troublemakers to the mouths of cannons and blowing them to pieces. In the Indian Army that was the traditional punishment. However, although it had been inherited from the Indians themselves, it did nothing to inspire loyalty. Amazingly, despite this unrest, the British government allowed the ratio of British to Indian troops within the sub-continent to decline from 1:3 to 1:6.

In 1857, for those who were prepared to look for them, the signs were there that the sepoys were deeply unhappy, and their officers had not the ability to prevent minor mutinies, only to deal with them when they occurred. They no longer participated in the sepoys' festivals, no longer spent time talking to their NCOs. They were cut off in their own lines, more concerned with their memsahibs than their troops. If there was a mutiny on the way they were in no position to foresee it or forestall it, and in 1857 a major mutiny was most certainly on its way.

The year of 1857 found Lang in Northern India, at Lahore, the chief city of the Punjab. He was the Executive Engineer, Public Works Department, of the Mian Mir Division. It was not a glamorous job, but in fact he could scarcely have landed a more interesting appointment.

The Punjab was the land of the Sikhs — Indians who had since the sixteenth century practised a religion that owed something to both Hinduism and Islam, while also professing much the same moral and domestic virtues as Christianity. Significantly it prohibited the caste system and the practice of suttee. Not unnaturally Hindus therefore despised the Sikhs, and Sikhs hated the Hindus.

For decades the rulers of the Punjab were happy for it to act as a buffer state between British India and the warlike Afghan tribes, but when British prestige was severely dented by defeats in the Afghan War of 1838-42, the Sikhs decided to attack the British troops on the frontier. This First Sikh War ended in 1846, following a crushing defeat of the Sikhs. However, the Governor-General still refrained from outright annexation. Instead he appointed one of his most able administrators, Henry Lawrence (himself, by training, an army officer), to the post of British Resident at Lahore, to safeguard British interests and re-establish self-government.

Lawrence was totally committed to this policy, but when he went home on sick leave in 1848 there was a fresh outbreak of violence. This time British victory was followed by annexation. The Governor-General realized that this could only succeed if he sent to this vast new province the very best men he had available. For some time it was to be run by a triumvirate: the Lawrence brothers, Henry and John — both brilliant administrators, but often bitterly divided over what policy to administer — with, as peacemaker, Robert Montgomery (grandfather of the Field-Marshal).

ARTHUR LANG (1808-1883)
Lang's father, a man of liberal ideals and conservative Christian convictions, was a distinguished judge in the EIC. Though by then retired to Westhill in Harrow, he was one of the few civilians quoted in Malleson's history of the Mutiny. His son inherited his sympathy with the Indian people – a sympathy shattered for a time by the Mutiny but soon restored. To their surprise perhaps, judge and soldier would be recognised by their descendants as very similar personalities – kindly, gifted, but ultimately unambitious, Christian gentlemen.

This triumvirate typified all that was best in British administration and in its administrators. All three were men of outstanding ability, and totally devoted to India and its peoples. Their Christianity was, like that of most of their contemporaries, imbued with an Old Testament fervour, stern and unforgiving, but always as demanding on themselves as it was on others. All three had been raised — again like so many others who would distinguish themselves during the Mutiny — in the stern protestant tradition of Northern Ireland, a land that has given Britain an exceptionally large number of its best military leaders.

The triumvirate certainly produced miracles for the Punjab, but it took considerable toll of the triumvirs, who wore themselves out in its service. By 1857 it had been disbanded. Henry Lawrence had been appointed Chief Commissioner of Oudh, Sir John was now sole Chief Commissioner of the Punjab, and Montgomery its Judicial Commissioner. These were supported by other men of exceptional ability whom the Lawrences had attracted to the Punjab, many of them like Robert Napier, Alex Taylor, and (far more junior) Arthur Lang, all military engineers, who in the Public Works Department were responsible for a crash programme for building roads, canals and camps for what was in effect an army of occupation.

Lang was simply a junior executive officer at the time, but he had considerable responsibilities: the maintenance of the cantonment [barracks] of Mian Mir, some five miles from the city of Lahore, as well as for all engineering works in the city of Lahore and in the British administrative enclave of Anarkullie which lay between the two. The work was hard, but it was typical of the duties undertaken by young Bengal Engineer officers of that time. What made it more interesting than most appointments was that Lahore was at the very centre of the administration of what was to prove the key province in the year of the Mutiny.

It was Lang's second appointment, and he had been there since August, 1856. The life he followed was typical of life in an Indian station. He would be up by six, out for a ride (often on his new horse, Herat, a 'vicious' animal of which he was gradually 'proving himself the master'), followed perhaps by a visit to one of the regimental coffee shops [a social gathering over an early breakfast], then work, either in his little office in Lahore or in Mian Mir, from about seven until two, broken only by a mid-morning breakfast. After tiffin [light luncheon], his afternoon would be taken up by reading, practising on his clarionet or teaching himself the concertina. He would dine (the main meal of the day) in the late afternoon either in his own house, or more often as a guest at one of the regimental messes or one of the families at Mian Mir or Anarkullie.

In the early evening he would always take some physical exercise, either racquets or gymnastics at which he was clearly the station's star. Later he would go to listen to one of the regimental bands, and ride perhaps on the Mall in the middle of camp with a group of young officers and 'Ladies' (His use of the capital letter was significant. He and his fellow officers carried their formal respect for the women of their social circle almost to religious extremes.). He was an eligible young man and many officers and administrators had daughters or sisters staying with them on the station. Lang's name was apparently often linked with one or another of the marriageable ladies, but he assured his family he had no intention of marrying till he next came home on leave, and that could not be for many years yet.

The chief excitements of life in Mian Mir were made up of rumours of romance, or of who was at church each Sunday, or when the punkahs [fans] would first be used or the ice pits opened. Apart from the occasional broadside from Sir John Lawrence demanding why Lang had not yet sorted out his predecessor's accounts (Sir John was notorious for chasing his engineers, whom he considered spendthrift, and Lang had apparently inherited a chaotic set of accounts!), life at Mian Mir was as good as any energetic young subaltern could wish for — or it was until 12 May.

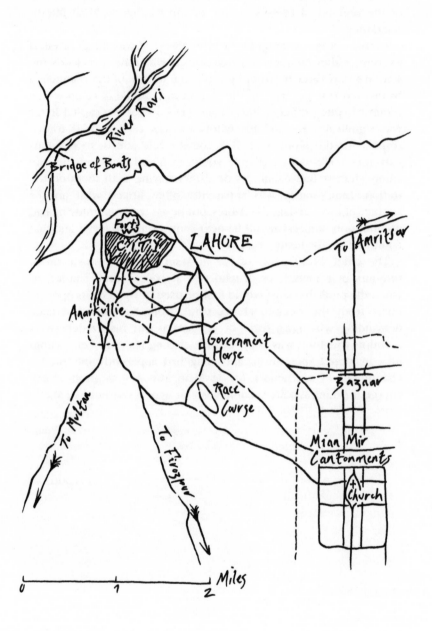

LAHORE, 1857

CHAPTER 2

The Devil's Wind

In 1857 the cantonment of Mian Mir was garrisoned by a fairly typical mixture of British (Queen's) and Indian troops. The Indian Army supplied the great majority: the 16th, 26th and 49th Native Infantry, the 8th Cavalry, and four companies of Bengal Foot Artillery. Only the 81st (Queen's) Foot, and two troops of the Bengal Horse Artillery were units of the British Army.

In May, 1857, the senior officers were Brigadier Corbett (in command of the station in the absence of General Gowan), Colonel Boileau (who commanded the artillery) and Colonel Smith (who commanded the 81st Foot). Others at the station with whom Arthur Lang was especially friendly were Captain Robert Wroughton of the Commissariat Department, Lieutenant Frank Boileau of the 16th Native Infantry (N.I.), and Lang's engineering colleagues and assistants: 'Ski' Gustavinski, D. Kerwan, and Lieutenant Henry Gulliver. His closest friend, 2nd-Lieutenant Elliot Brownlow, had just left for Kashmir on an intelligence mission for Sir John Lawrence.

Although in the first months of 1857 there had been reports of unrest throughout the army in Bengal, especially over the issue of the new cartridges, this had not caused much concern in Lahore. After all, scarcely a year went by without reports of unrest somewhere within the Indian Army, and most outbreaks were dealt with promptly by executing a few ringleaders. So at Mian Mir all was quiet, or so it seemed to Lang as he wrote his journal on the morning of 12 May.

12 May 1857, Mian Mir Nothing particular has happened. Yesterday I visited works and messes in the morning; worked and played the clarionet and concertina in the day, gymnastics and a lounge at the Band in the evening, and dined at Wroughton's. I heard from Elliot Brownlow that he was going to make his start for Kagan in a few days.

5pm. Since I wrote the above, I have heard some very less pleasant intelligence, really very bad. You know, tho' I don't think I have touched much upon it, that a mutinous spirit has been pervading the Bengal Regiments: that at Dinajpur, Lucknow, Meerut, Phillaur and Ambala, regiments have been either mutinying or burning. Well today I have just heard from Ambala that two Native Infantry regiments mutinied to save some of their comrades imprisoned for not using the greased cartridges. The Artillery and Cavalry were called out and the regiments gave up their arms and returned to barracks.

Now comes up a flying telegraphic message: Meerut barracks burned, men risen and have *murdered* their officers, regiments ordered to rescue have refused. The Phillaur regiment has made a move to seize the Sutlej bridge of boats, and an Artillery company march to Phillaur from here tomorrow. Here comes our danger. The Brigadier is going to disarm the native troops tomorrow here! This is a fearfully responsible act: tomorrow morning is to be a full parade, the Europeans and Artillery will be loaded, and who knows but that the three Native Infantry and the Cavalry Regiment won't fight? They have done nothing yet, have shown no signs of disaffection.

Were I Brigadier I should draw them up, commend their fine state of discipline, point out the folly and wickedness of their brother sepoys, and confide entirely in their honour and loyalty to stand by their officers and Government. As it is, with this disarming, I expect they will rise. Where is this to end? I can't believe that the Anglo-Saxon is going to be turned out of India, but a feather's weight more on the scale and down it will go.

Tonight, too, we all go to a Ball hardly one knowing the volcano we are here standing over, none perhaps but the Brigadier, Brigade Major, Wroughton, the Colonels, and I, and poor Mrs Brigadier who is nearly wild with fright. Wroughton says that Mr Montgomery has come up to point out the danger of a spark causing the population about here to rise. God grant they don't and that we are all alive this time tomorrow: a case of both guns loaded with ball and my swords at the head of my bed tonight. Even if the men, from pressure of Artillery and Europeans, yield their arms, what is to secure us from plotting and conspiracy and murder of all of us tomorrow night or the next!

I am helping Wroughton to collect all the carriage he can get to carry off the arms after parade tomorrow: the Europeans are to escort these to the Fort. Four companies of the 81st take possession of that tomorrow. I wish the 81st were stronger: they were much weakened by the cholera last year. God help us! There is really no telling where all this will end. Goodbye dearest Mother for the present . . . .

Just back from the Ball and will finish and close this in case of accidents. The evening has passed very pleasantly – a perfect sham of smiles over tears. Half the Ladies were not present and those who were there could barely disguise their anxiety, while we gentlemen had to give the brightest picture of the case possible, tho' they must often have heard pieces of subdued conversations anything but hopeful.

In fact we know exactly what it is. Here are two regiments of Native Infantry, a wing of a third, and a regiment of Cavalry, before six companies of the 81st and two troops of Horse Artillery. Will they, innocent men, consent to give up their arms? I doubt it. I think a volley will be their reply, and how will that matter end? All their officers are indignant and fully trust their regiments, but of course once disarmed they will become disaffected. Three hours hence it will be over, one way or another. God grant that there be no bloodshed.

I hope all these dreadful matters will end before the mail goes out, or you will all at home be in such anxiety about us. Well, goodnight dearest Mother. I think that I had better have an hour's sleep.

13 May We are all safe at present you see, and this morning's work went off without any rising, but still of course we don't know yet what may happen.

I have been asleep nearly all day, as I got none last night but was in the saddle at daybreak with the Brigadier and his staff. This morning the Horse Artillery drew up their formidable lines of black muzzles pointing on to the grand parade, cantonment at their back. The 81st, only six companies, drew up behind the guns, the 16th, 26th, 49th, and 8th Cavalry, in contiguous columns facing this line (about 350 or 400 yds off). The Brigadier soft-sawdered them, saying what splendid regiments they were, how he loved them, how he longed to win their further honour and to keep their name unsullied, and so he was going to order them to show their loyalty in laying down their arms.

We were riding within a few yards of the line and could see every face and hear every murmur; but not a sound. Then came the critical moment. 'Order the 16th to pile arms.' I looked at the unfortunate N.I. officers amongst their men. We could have escaped with but one volley, for we were on horseback and could have joined the Horse Artillery: but what would they have done?

'Grenadiers, shoulder arms.' Done. 'Ground arms.' Done. 'Pile arms.' A moment's hesitation, a few men began to pile; a look at the black Artillery muzzles must have been decisive: all piled arms. 'Stand from your arms .... Right about face .... Quick march.' Away they went unarmed, the clusters of bayonets glittering under the morning sun, marking where they had stood and showing their obedience (under pressure perhaps). Of course, after this the 26th and 49th followed suit in turn, and the Cavalry dropped swords and backed out of them: then up came the carts, and the arms were carried off. I galloped to where in the distance the Foot Artillery were drawn up, useless tailors without their guns. There old Boileau, revolver in belt, was beginning to look cheerful, and poor Mrs Boileau and the Misses were waiting anxiously to hear of 'dear Frank' in the Grenadiers.

So far, thank God, it is all well, but are we really safe? If these men get maddened (for this is a disgrace, however much soft-sawder the Brigadier may give) and choose to run amuck among us, they will have done awful mischief before they can be stopped. They are very much cut up about it and declare that they would at once, on their own parades, have obeyed orders and given up their arms, but they are very much hurt at the loaded guns and the Europeans being drawn up against them. We must be thankful that no *émeute* took place this morning and trust that all may end well.

I really expect we shall have to spend the hot months in Fort, or send for the 61st (Queen's) from Firozpur. Artillery and Infantry pickets and patrols are all over the station and no natives are allowed to move after sunset. I am going to dine at the 16th mess tonight.

I wonder whether we or you by the time this mail goes out will manage to hear what has happened at Delhi: it seems doubtful whether we shall be able to receive or send letters. The impression is that all the Xtian population have been murdered, and the people here, but more particularly in Anarkullie, dread the same game being played here. Never, I fancy, was so dangerous a disaffection in the Indian Army before. I hope, dearest Mother, the post and telegraph will be in play again before next mail goes out, or you will be very anxious if you hear the Delhi and Meerut news.

14 May In the morning I went across to the 49th Mess to hear the news and then to Wroughton's. I stayed to breakfast there. As Wroughton and I were discussing the *only* topic, in ran the scared servants − 'Sahibs, the regiments are up and collecting on the maidan [open plain] to march on Lahore.'

Off went Wroughton with a buggy full of swords etc. to the 81st barracks. I walked out without horse or arms, and joined a detachment of Europeans, marching along, their bayonets gleaming under something like a sun. I had sent for horse and sword, but was until their arrival rather a useless party with an umbrella! As we approached the Artillery lines up galloped the Brigadier saying the alarm was false: the men were bolting to the villages about. So back we marched.

The Horse Artillery had turned out in less than no time, anyhow, wild to have a brush with the Cavalry who they supposed were coming at them. The Artillery Ladies all fled in tears and fright to the Artillery hospital. The Fort fired their warning guns: out from all the offices filed the sahibs, double-barrels in hands, and rode for the Fort: clerks all bolted to the central jail. The Anarkullie Ladies are in the Fort! Mrs Corbett, who should have had a dinner party and fed me last night, won't come out of the Artillery hospital at any price! The Montgomerys alone stand firm in their isolated place and quite right they are too, I think. I wonder whether their guests will go tomorrow night: I will (D.V.).

Well, what did the men after all? Evil-disposed scoundrels had been working on the feelings of the mass that the cartridges should certainly be issued this morning; they are unarmed and therefore helpless: they would have the alternative, 'Eat or be blown to pieces!' So they began bolting: but I fancy by the evening they were all back again, their officers, the Brigadier etc. having been perpetually with them, arguing and bringing them to reason.

I dined at Wroughton's and slept there, preferring that locale to mine in the very midst of the 49th and 16th men's lines.

15 May This morning I have been here, my little office, writing and playing concertina. The inhabitants of Lahore City are in such a jolly panic; my baboos [clerks] have been imploring to be let off early, as they didn't eat anything this morning, in such terror of the sepoys rising.

I wish we could get some news from Meerut and Ambala. Telegraphic news is just in that at Jhelum a Movable Column is to be formed to move instantly to any spot showing disaffection. We have also an express from Firozpur: 45th and 57th N.I. have mutinied; the 10th Cavalry stood by Government. The 10th and the 61st (Queen's) broke and dispersed them.

I don't know how it is that I can't feel the danger as it ought to be felt; I'm either apathetic or stupid about it — tho' not apathetic, for I feel occasionally the *pleasure* of the excitement. I pity the poor Ladies, their fears for kith and kin. I stand *alone* to risk it.

16 May Another day well on, and we are all going on comfortably. I dined

last night at the Montgomerys, and all his party (I fancy) came. We had a pleasant enough evening, music etc. The Anarkullie ladies and Keraniesses [female Eurasians] are now in the Fort. The civilians and our Engineer, Gulliver, sleep in a tent by Mr Montgomery's. Sowar [cavalry] patrols guard all the roads. Twenty rupees a head have been offered for all deserters brought in. All the men who bolted from here have been heard of and will be captured.

They say that in Delhi the officer in charge of the arsenal laid a charge of gunpowder, and stood hours match in hand. When a grand mass of ruffians had poured in, he blew them and himself up. The 3rd Cavalry at Meerut killed their colonel by shutting him up in his house and burning him to death. Oh the fiends! How one longs for the most cruel and fearful retribution to fall on them! They killed Ladies too, the cowards: cutting through the station during evening service on Sunday, sabring unfortunate women. It makes one mad to think of it! I wonder what is going on down country in that Poorbya [east of the Punjab] country denuded of European troops. I can't but think that Cawnpore, Allahabad, Benares etc. will follow the Delhi game. A campaign in June and July will kill the Europeans. If we survive this, never will a Hindustani be enlisted again, I suppose. Our army should be entirely European, Afghan, Gurkha and Sikh.

18 May Here are Ski and I alive and jolly in my house, not yet cut up, our guns, swords and revolvers ready to pick up at any moment. This is truly an exciting time, but I find it suits me beautifully. I feel always in very good spirits, sleep like a top, have a grand appetite, and forget it is the hot weather. In fact the state of things, I am very happy to find, braces me up instead of depressing me or unstringing my nerves. The result shows me that a campaign would suit me, a fact I was not sure of, for I am very excitable on many subjects and fighting is one. But I find that actual danger, or expectation of it, calms and 'irons' me at once. We had two alarms yesterday and I expect every hour to hear more.

On Saturday [16 May] Ski and I dined at 26th mess. Afterwards we paid the centre picket a visit. The Brigadier and most of the staff had their charpoys [beds] there and sleep there. In fact, we were ordered to do so, but I did not join the picket until last night.

Yesterday was Sunday, but no holiday for me. I had represented to the Brigadier that I had upwards of 30,000 rupees Government treasure, and that my guard of havildar [Indian sergeant] and eight (sepoys of course) are only armed with bayonets. He ordered me to get it away as best I could. Of course, no European guard could be spared, so I got two elephants, took a rezai [counterpane] off my bed, put 15,000 rupees just anyhow into it, and flung the bundle carelessly on one elephant; a durree [carpet] on the other side held another 15,000, and off I sent them at 9 am. I followed in a buggy.

I called on Mr Montgomery to know where to lodge the monies and he referred me to the Fort. He told me that orders for levying 7000 Sikhs, horse and foot, had come. Also that Anson [Commander-in-Chief, India] had written to say that he was afraid to move from Ambala because of the mutinous spirit of the two N.I. regiments. Just fancy! 9th Lancers, 75th (Queen's), 1st and 2nd Fusiliers, European Horse Artillery, and he funks! Mr Montgomery had written to urge him very strongly to order both regiments on parade, and order them to march into the jail and, if they refuse, instanter to blow them to pieces. Similar advice had been given to Brigadier Innes at Firozpur, anent the 45th and 57th, at least the 700 of them who are there, the rest having deserted. I hope these will, like firm men, act promptly.

I took my elephants to the Fort, and lodged my money there. The Fort is of course being armed and victualled for siege. I visited the Dr, and found six Ladies with their children there: some going daft with fright, even in that safe place, guarded by high walls and Europeans. I heard such stories of the flight into the Fort, how Ladies came eight or nine in a carriage, and ran into the gateways, their children in their arms!

In the afternoon I drove back well roasted and slept. Of course, there was no service in church, but I went over to the Artillery barracks where Farrer [Chaplain, Mian Mir] read service to the Artillerymen under arms in the open air. In the evening I dined with Farrer. Several dropped in after dinner, and as we chatted, 'Hullo, the Assembly! The Alarm! By Jove, the Double! The troops must be up.' Out we sallied to the centre picket, which of course was under arms, portfires burning, men at the guns. Off rode the Brigadier and some more, and presently rode back to say that our foemen were some thirty Indian sabres: allies, sowars sent up by the civilians. As they had come tearing in at full gallop on a pitch dark night they had startled the picket at the 81st end.

Ski and I slept at the picket. It was very jolly, regularly martial, calling of sentries, neighing of horses, clanking of arms, and the knowledge that we were all in earnest, every weapon loaded. Sleeping out on the plain, under the beautiful starlit sky, in the midst of all this pomp of war, was very pleasant. I slept, as I always do, like a top, and at about 2 was shaken out of senses nearly by my bearer: 'Stand to your arms!' I felt very inclined to go on sleeping, and was disgusted to hear, as I was buckling on my sword, that it was all false again. The sepoys are in an awful fright of us and we of them apparently: it does seem skittles:

35

the sepoys will presently be goaded by sheer anxiety and fright to end the suspense by running amuck.

Half the Ladies are quartered in the centre Artillery barrack and half in the centre 81st. Poor creatures! Some of them are so frightened: last night one Artillery woman screamed: a lot, of course, out of sympathy joined and they and the Ladies got wild, hid under the beds.

The N.I. officers are in the most critical position, for their duty is to go to their men's lines if any row occurs, and they know what risk that is. Next door to me, about fourteen of the 49th have put Captain Larkins's house in a state of defence. They have some 70 guns in the house, and two are always on guard. I suppose I should make over there if I see a party of sepoys dashing up to my door; precious little chance of escape, however, I expect.

19 May Yesterday Ski and I went to see Mrs Boileau, and stopped for dinner. I went to Wroughton's in the evening and found him poor fellow very miserable at the news from Simla. The Nusseerie battalion, close to Simla, refused to march when ordered and became riotous. You know the Gurkhas, fiery and brave little fellows in fight, but little cruel demons. You may imagine how anxious all people are whose friends are in Simla. Poor Wroughton, with his wife, three little children, two sisters, and a sister-in-law up there — almost all he cares for — has been intensely unhappy. He cannot get news from Delhi or Meerut. I do hope we hear they are all safe.

A very pleasant day today! I was told off for special duty: first to go up and examine the church belfry and report its capabilities as a watch-tower, and then I was ordered to spend the day there and take Gustavinski, Frank Boileau and one of my overseers. Who should appear in the station and at my house but my old chum Edward Salwey, whom I had not seen for nearly five years: an unlucky time for him to make his appearance, but I was delighted to see him, and he joined our belfry party.

The belfry is a square room, entered through the floor by a wooden trap door and into which such luxuries as chairs and tables could not be got. The eight long gothic windows were furnished only with slate venetians. From each window I had a slate taken out, and with our telescopes, our cards and books, rezais and naunds [earthenware pots] of water, stocked with bottles of beer, soda water and lemonade, we spent a most jolly day, tho' the heat was intense. The sun roasting this little square chamber, whose windows were unclosed, made it like an oven. The thermometer must have been nearly 120 degrees, and we were like so many Strasbourg geese preparing ourselves for pâté de foie gras. Didn't we consume drinkables! We saw nothing all day, either in the station which lay below us, as deserted and silent as a city of the dead, or in the country round, which also lay asleep under the winking haze of heat.

Sunset relieved us from our burning prison. We dined at the 16th mess, and slept at the picket. We had tops of tents pitched at the picket and under one of these I slept. So cold is it at night — rezais and blankets.

21 May Yesterday our state of siege was made stricter. All the Ladies were quartered off in barracks, and officers ordered to keep to their own lines. I ignore this imprisonment order. In the evening Ski and I rode to the Artillery barracks, and saw all the Ladies there sitting outside their barracks to breathe a little fresh air. We stopped some time chatting with the Boileaus, then went to the 16th mess, played pool etc., and then again to picket.

Today Kerwan made his appearance at 16th Coffee Shop in the khaki coat, trowsers and puggree [light turban] of the Volunteers. All the Xtians in Anarkullie, commissioners and clerks, have formed a Brook Green Militia [a creation of *Punch*]. Gulliver is adjutant, and drills them morning and evening. I rode down the desolate Mall and dined at 26th Mess. No great event happened, except that the ice pits were opened, and that is matter of no small importance.

22 May The state of excitement is itself becoming monotonous. We want some more earnest work to keep up the fire. We remain as quiet as possible, each side mutually afraid of the other, but as we are armed and the four Native regiments have only their tulwars [sabres] and lathis [sticks], I think we at least should not feel the fear which some of our nervous parties indulge in. The Ladies are safely secured in barracks (and don't the dear creatures quarrel!).

They say the Nusseerie battalion is now all ready to march, and quite quiet. A European regiment is ordered up from Karachi to Firozpur, and steamers are sent out to intercept the China-bound troops. Agra, Moradabad, Aligarh, all safe on the 10th. We cannot get certain news from either Delhi or Meerut: at the latter the Europeans are supposed to be entrenched, while all the natives have gone over to Delhi; but whether the Meerut N.I. have killed all their officers we know not; or whether the 38th and 74th officers at Delhi have all been killed, as well as the 54th.

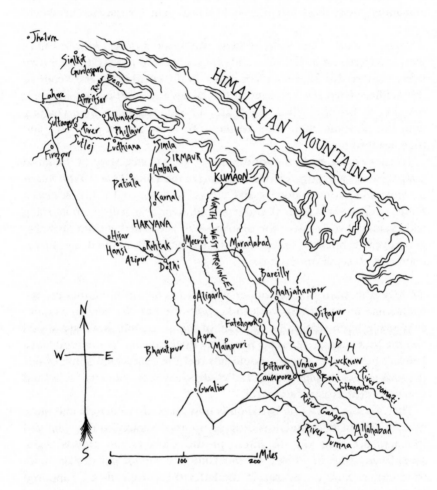

NORTHERN INDIA, 1857

38

CHAPTER 3

Waiting for the Word

At Lahore Lang had far from complete information on what had happened elsewhere in India, but he and his colleagues soon grasped the essentials: the loss of Delhi, Sir Henry Lawrence under siege in Lucknow, and the mutiny of almost every sepoy regiment in the Bengal Army. Of the major disasters only the massacre of Cawnpore remained undiscovered for some time. The Rebellion, as they called it then, was indeed the greatest threat yet to British rule in India. It was, however, confined to northern India – Bengal, the North-West Provinces, Oudh and the Punjab.

Unfortunately for the British, not all military commanders had acted as decisively as Brigadier Corbett at Lahore. Most had also 'soft-sawdered' their troops, but unlike Corbett not all had disarmed them. Sooner or later their sepoys mutinied, either massacring their British officers or simply leaving their barracks and going off to join their fellows in Delhi.

Delhi, once capital of the old Moghul empire, was for both Moslems and Hindus the national heart of India. Without control of Delhi, Britain could not pretend to control the sub-continent. The Indians realized this; so did the British. For the British, however, there was a major problem. They had no leader on the spot. The Governor-General, Lord Canning, a newcomer to India, was stranded out of touch in Calcutta. The Commander-in-Chief, General Anson, was dying of cholera. His immediate successors, Generals Barnard and Reed, were inexperienced and elderly. The only man with the energy and experience required was Sir John Lawrence in the Punjab. He acted immediately. He decided to gamble everything on regaining Delhi as fast as possible.

He began by creating the Movable (mobile) Column, and put in charge of it his most gifted (though far from most senior) officers:

first Neville Chamberlain, and then, when Chamberlain was needed at Delhi, John Nicholson. Nicholson's exploits as a commander against the hill tribes of the Afghan border had won him the status there of a demi-god, and one sect even worshipped him as 'Nikal Seyn'. An austere protestant from Northern Ireland, Nicholson was appalled by this reaction, and ordered his followers to be flogged. Their devotion only increased. More importantly, Nicholson's superiors and his troops admired him just as much — as a military leader, at any rate. He was a commander waiting for his moment. It had come.

The odds against the British were, of course, appallingly long. It would be months before fresh troops could come from England, though a few of those on their way to fight in China would be diverted to Calcutta. Admittedly there was no sign yet of the Mutiny spreading to Southern India, but only a few of the regiments there could be spared to help the north. The only hope was to raise troops among the very troops that the British had been fighting a few years before — the Sikhs themselves. This Lawrence now set out to do, creating 'Irregular' regiments either by raising them in the Punjab or from among any Sikhs or Afghans there might be in the disbanded sepoy regiments. As the Sikhs and Afghans liked nothing better than the thought of sacking a few Hindu cities, Lawrence's policy was a resounding success. The main problem was one of time. He must get results quickly or these fierce tribesmen would decide that the British could never regain control. Then they would at best drift home, and at worst turn once again on the British.

In a desperate gamble to seize Delhi as quickly as possible, Lawrence decided to denude his own province of the very troops it might need for its own security. Lang welcomed the policy and imagined he would be among the first to go. He was not. Day after day his diary and journal were filled with news of action from Delhi, of how tension at Lahore fluctuated, with the families kept sometimes in barracks day and night and sometimes only overnight, and of his irritation at his own position. He was less forthcoming, however, about another development that was to compensate him for some of that irritation.

2 June Last night in came some of the Movable Column: the 52nd (Queen's), some Artillery and Punjab Cavalry. The 52nd, their jackets, trowsers and cap covers dyed khaki, look very soldierly.

This morning I was surprised to see guns tearing along and taking up commanding position at curious crossroads: presently out rang the Horse Artillery trumpets and in dashed a crowd of troopers and guns into the 8th Cavalry lines and swept out the horses. It was done very neatly and as fast as I write it. The 8th Cavalry, who have caused such a lot of false reports and such alarm to our croaking cowards, but who I fancy are as non-disaffected as any nigger regiment can be, certainly have not much chance of doing much harm. The sepoys don't know what goes on: I expect they fear being charged and blown up now that more Artillery and Infantry have come in.

5 June Yesterday I went over after office hours to the Boileaus, where Mrs Rumley, Miss Boileau and I — two concertinas and a clarionet — had a wonderful concert. Rode on the Mall with them in the evening, and returned to their 'Ice' tea afterwards, till they retired to barracks.

7 June We are all jolly here. Anarkullie is like a great fair now, full of troops from the Column. The bands play again in the evening and people are much more courageous. Farrer performed service in church this morning to about 40; of course the troops don't come.

Sikhs, Hillmen and Punjabis, from the 16th, 26th and 49th, are to be picked out, to march to Lahore this afternoon, to receive arms and be formed into a Depot. We have had heavy dust storms followed by rain: it almost seems as if the rains were coming on. If they are, I must say that we have had no hot weather to speak of. When the hot weather first came on I thought that I should want the hills, which supported me last year and the year before, but I find that I don't suffer from the heat. In fact, I find myself sitting an hour or two without having the punkah pulled.

9 June Those idiotic Jullundur regiments have risen. Neville Chamberlain and his Column are to be off in pursuit this evening. I shall not be sorry when the Column is off, for I think a great part of it is more to be looked on as foes than friends.

I wish I could hear from you and get my letters, but patience must ever be the word. I think I must make up a bundle of letters and send them off to Karachi, for transmission to England, before the Multan troops rise and stop our only road for English letters. The Eastern road is closed again, telegraphs cut, and daks [mails] stopped.

12 June Before the Column marched, Chamberlain had two of the 35th blown away from the guns for mutinous language. I then received the pleasant order to have gallows erected to accommodate twelve men at once. Never having seen a gallows with its paraphernalia of drops etc., my contrivances are original if nothing else. Courts martial sit every day. The first day they condemned eleven men to be hung, but General Gowan (this blind idiotic leniency again which made the 3rd Cavalry rise and begin the whole row) reprieved them and commuted sentences to fourteen, ten etc. years imprisonment.

14 June Please thank Aunt Mary for the pretty set of cricketing studs: very novel and calculated to produce no end of a sensation next cricket Ladies' tiffin. When shall we play cricket again? We are sending Foot Artillery men from here to Delhi. I am sending doolies [litters] to Multan for the Bombay Fusiliers, who are coming up here. Then off will go the 81st to Delhi.

We get now long interesting letters of what happened at Meerut and Delhi, but one is choked with indignation at the cruelty with which the poor women have been treated. I hope no quarter, no mercy, will be the cry when we have the upper hand. Don't fear the result. 'Britons never shall be slaves,' etc., and we are not going to be kicked out of India if every native regiment and every black Rajah and Nawab rises against us; it comes to a religious war of Christians versus Mohammedans and Hindus, and we know which must win.

17 June This morning the mail has arrived without any warning, any *avant-couriers* of telegraphic messages; every wire which isn't cut has too much to tell about the Rebellion to *waste* time over English mails. Come along tho', English mails, and bring us out some more stout hands and hearts, for it is all we can do to hold our own: the pressure is becoming heavy: our enemies increase daily, fresh barbarities happen, and no reinforcements can come to our poor army before Delhi.

Yesterday news was bad, for it tells the strength of our enemy: every day at Delhi they come out and every day have our poor fellows to fight through the hottest hours. On the 15th out came the enemy and got his usual licking, back marched our wearied troops and just as they piled arms, fresh alarms sounded! The enemy, a new and fresh batch, were out again, and off went our worn-out soldiers to fight again. They were fighting when the message left.

I broke up the bridge of boats yesterday to stop the ingress of the 14th (Jhelum) and the 46th (Sialkot) who are expected to rise.

18 June Chamberlain is Adjutant General, and Nicholson — the stern, the dreaded and the worshipped of the wild frontier enemy — is to command

JOHN LAWRENCE (1811-1879)
Son of a soldier, and brother of four soldiers (all of whom became
generals), John Lawrence rose through the Indian Civil Service to surpass
them all, becoming the first Lord Lawrence and Viceroy of India. A brilliant
administrator, though less inspirational than his brother Henry, who was
to die at Lucknow, John had the gift of inexhaustible energy. He harried
his engineers in the Punjab — both Taylor and Lang learned to dread his
visits — but without his grim resolve in 1857 Britain would certainly have
lost Northern India.

the Movable Column. We have no more news from Delhi: tho' we have more details, which the editors ought to be prevented from publishing, considering that poor frightened Ladies all read. I tore paragraphs out of mine before lending them. Our soldiers who know these things are quite mad and want to stick every native they see.

Mother, one month of India now would change your opinion of a lifetime. We on the spot can hear of nothing every day but base ingratitude and deceit, and fiendish cruelty. You'll not say 'the mild inoffensive Hindu' again! Let us forget India and its dear population, and none of your chaff now about ye trials of ye domestic bachelor! I scorn to write for the eighth time the genealogy of Col Boileau! No, I won't tell any more about where you knew him, or of his wife, a very pleasant ladylike kind of person, or of Mademoiselles Sarah and Grace, or of Frank Boileau, a Lieut in the 16th Grenadiers, or of Charlie in Hill's 61st, or four more boys − 2 at home and 2 cheeky youngsters out here, who call me 'Lang' and otherwise irritate me! So you needn't ask any more questions about them.

21 June It is believed that the Gwalior Contingent have joined the rebels. If so, all Central India must have gone. Our acquisition of the Punjab seems to be our saving. Here alone we stand fast, and from here we send regiment after regiment to win back Hindustan proper for us. The Sikhs, Gurkhas and Afghans delight in going down to loot Hindustan. The Guides who were left to look after the women etc. of the regiment have bolted − not to leave us but to get to Delhi! They are determined to join in the sack.

22 June I am running up partition walls in the Ladies' barracks: these as you may fancy are troublesome, Ladies being given to think others better off than themselves.

23 June The 100th anniversary of Plassey. I wonder if they will assault and take Delhi today. I hope not, for I want to be there. I have volunteered for Delhi. Both Macpherson [Military Secretary to Sir John Lawrence] and Montgomery seem to approve, so I shall soon devise a bundle of the most useful articles up to 20 seers weight [40 lbs] and make arrangements for leaving my work and property in good hands here. No end of roughing, for I can't take anything with me, tents, servants, horses or anything; just a bundle I can carry, rattle off as best I can and get what shelter I can find.

I hope I may be in time. What a change − heat and fighting and fatigue − to this luxurious dawdling cantonment life. I dare say I shall wish myself back in Mme Boileau's drawing room, playing 'La ci darem' and such like, with her daughter Sarah. But I am right, don't you think so, in volunteering? This is no time for men to be idling and shirking; help is greatly wanted in Delhi, and I shall be much more useful there than I am here in inglorious ease and security.

25 June Here I am still, bad luck to it! I am very nearly in the fashionable suicide condition. I volunteered on Monday [22 June]; on Tuesday Mr Montgomery said he would let me know, in the course of the day. I wait in suspense, make up khaki trowsers, tunics, and turbans, in the most hasty manner and imagine myself at Delhi in less than no time. To relieve my excitement, I galloped about cantonments and saw Salwey (lucky dog!) and his Artillerymen start for Amritsar.

Yesterday, of course, I thought for certain that I should mount the mail-cart at half-past one: not a bit of it. I got Sir John's answer: 'I will enquire if Lt Lang is required: don't send him yet.' And so it stands and I shall not go, or, if I do, I shall be late for the fighting, only in time for fever and cholera and demolishing the walls of Delhi in the rains. To preserve myself from suicide I went over to Col Boileau's and stayed there till they went to barracks.

27 June I have no further news about my going or not going. The weather is delightful − 10am, 88 degrees, all doors open, no punkahs etc., merry sunshine, clear atmosphere and cloudy sky − a regular change from hot weather to rains. You must be just receiving my first letter after the breaking out of the Rebellion. I hope you will not have been alarmed about me. In reality I have been very happy and comfortable here − too much so, I feel, while my countrymen in other stations have been so harassed and injured. I wish I could get my orders to be off: this would be a gloriously cool day to mount the mail-cart, but I begin to despair of being allowed to go.

30 June I have not yet got orders to go. I am all ready to be off at a minute's notice, and meanwhile go on in a careless, peaceful, station way, which I don't like, knowing that I have no right to be safe and comfortable, but being a strong young fellow, with nothing particular to do here, I should be doing my best in stern reality.

3 July A letter from Mrs Harris [wife of the Chaplain at Lucknow] has found its way here, dated 12 June, written in a very desponding strain, but reporting all as yet safe in the Residency, big guns pointing in all directions to protect them. She provokingly gives no list of the killed, nor news of the country about, except vague allusions to cruelties perpetrated in the out-stations. Sir Henry is blowing away and hanging all he manages to catch.

At Delhi it is reported that the assault will be given in a day or two; that powder is failing the enemy; that some of them daily desert; that the 19th N.I. en masse marched out homewards, was fired into by the rebels, and pursued by some of their cavalry; that General Barnard has died of cholera, and General Reed has taken command of the Army. General Barnard I am afraid is a great loss.

5 July I wish I could see your grounds at Westhill. How tantalising your description of grassy lawns, shady trees, spring breezes, azaleas, rhododendrons etc., sound to poor me, who looks out on the most scorched and brown of flat countries, almost invisible in the intense glare of a cloudless sky.

On 3 July came an order for Ski to take down 200 Mazbi [sweepers] Sikhs to join the Delhi Sappers. I certainly don't envy him; I wouldn't go down in that way for anything: he is collecting military necessaries. My tent and one of my swords are my contributions.

7 July How happy I am in having no relations out here (Dacres and Walter [Lang's cousins] are safe). So many have news to drive them mad. At Shahjahanpur nearly all the people were killed in church; those not in church escaped to a rajah who kept them, till the 28th advanced on him, and then he packed them off to Sitapur. En route they met the 41st who murdered them all.

I wish I were commanding here. I would take up the extermination policy advocated by *The Friend of India* [a weekly newspaper, published in Bengal], instead of keeping all the Europeans in a state of everlasting suspense and killing the women by inches. I'd have the whole native force out here and order them within a quarter of an hour to give me up ringleaders, one out of every ten men; otherwise volleys of grape and musketry should rid the station of these nightmares, and strike a gentle warning into the bosoms of troops at other stations. This long delay before Delhi has cost the lives of hundreds of our countrymen and women, and must lead, if still protracted, to the desertion of Sikhs, Punjabis and all who have not white faces.

There is a rumour, tho' how true we cannot say, that some four European regiments have got into the Doab [the land between the Ganges and the Jumna], that Sir Hugh Wheeler has put himself at their head, and attacked and thrashed a lot of mutinous regiments marching on Agra. Is it not odd that of all stations the one of which we know nothing (except its having been all nearly burned) is Cawnpore? Not one iota of news do we get from there.

8 July Last night we joined the European picket, being warned that it was unsafe to sleep in lines. The men that the Punjab battalion got from the 49th are going off tonight to Jullundur; they are not to be trusted here with their old regiment. The Punjab battalion is then to be made an Irregular Regiment and four officers left with it: Commandant (Larkins), 2nd in command, Adjutant, and, 'Doing duty', Frank Boileau.

10 July Here we are again in our 'siege' condition. All ladies secured in barracks, Larkins ordered to let his Sikhs fire into any party of natives numbering ten or more who may appear.

I have been all morning in their camp and challenged them all to athletic amusements — jumping, putting the shell etc. — and licked them. They are such jolly cool fellows these Sikhs, no cringing 'gharib parwaring' [Protector of the Poor' — a favourite Hindustani compliment], but they laugh and chaff at one in true manly style, and enter with a smile into the racing, games etc., and are very good natured, as I found when I 'put' a heavy shell on a fellow's foot!

Gustavinski and Kerwan are living with me now; we all sleep at the little European picket. I spent the afternoon at Col Boileau's and rode out again with Frank and his sisters. Dined at the 81st barracks. Well, goodbye for the present. I hope this letter, bungalow and all, won't be burnt presently. I don't think our regiments will be such fools as to rise with lathis and tulwars.

12 July All right you see. Yesterday morning Gustavinski marched from Anarkullie with his Mazbi Sikhs. I was out at the Artillery lines in the morning and saw the Bombay Fusiliers march in, all the women and ladies standing outside their barracks in great glee to see some more white faces (very sunburnt and dirty) with British hearts, hands and bayonets, come to defend them. On their arrival 100 of the 81st went off in ekkas [two-wheeled carts] for Amritsar.

We have had guns and European Infantry waiting at the bridge of boats for the Sialkot rebels, but they have made for Gurdaspur, where they will, I suppose, pick up the 2nd Irregulars. We had a detachment of that noble cavalry here, but their room being preferred to their company, they were told to go off to their own regiment yesterday.

As to my doings, they continue as if nothing was going on except that I do get rather pitched into for living in the 49th lines, tho' I sleep at the picket. Last night we were all roused by a horse rolling and a pistol in the holsters going off.

Yesterday Frank and I spent in barracks. Mrs Boileau's quarters are not so uncomfortable, being one of the end sergeant's quarters, so that they are much more private than parties who have little partitioned rooms in the big wards, with cutcha [rough] partition walls, only six feet high. These latter parties can't be very jolly and private. Mrs Boileau has one high centre room in which they sit by day and sleep by night, and two small verandah rooms and verandah beyond. They are shut out by high pukka [brick/proper] walls from their neighbours right and left.

You never had to live in barracks guarded night and day by sentries in your Indian career. *Voilà* the march of civilization! However, some of the Ladies keep up their spirits very well. Of course the horrible details which we hear with all these accounts of massacres etc., and which make the men's blood boil with indignation and hatred, distress poor women's minds and keep them perpetually miserable. You will feel horror enough, I dare say, but fancy the people living amidst it all, hearing these things every day, and knowing the sufferers in their widespread India acquaintanceship and hearing much more detail than you will. How very strange this state of things is whenever one thinks of it, but it has grown quite natural: it would be strange to hear of no disaster any day.

14 July Yesterday at daybreak the Brigadier drove me down to the river; we held a council as to the best way of defending the bridge. We saw the little force of a camp of 81st, and two guns on a sandy knoll on this bank of the river; precious hot little camp!

I was very miserable all day at Frank accepting the command of some Dogras [hill men from the north of the Punjab] going to Haryana. I am afraid he will soon be knocked up, and his mother and sisters will be so very anxious about him; it is bad for them having Charlie Boileau at Delhi.

Now goodbye. You will be thankful to see another fortnight has passed and that I am all safe: really there is *here* no cause for anxiety. Thanks (under God) to the very prompt measures taken by our Brigadier, Lahore has become, instead of a second Delhi, the rallying point of every native regiment in the Punjab, the British capital of Upper India, holding its own and helping the unfortunate North-West.

16 July I must send one sheet via Marseilles, just to tell you that this your son has found a darling little daughter-in-law (*in prospectu*) for you, and is intensely happy himself. I can't tell you more than that

SARAH BOILEAU (1838-1889)
Like most young officers, Lang expected to stay unmarried until his first
home leave, but early in 1857 he changed his mind: 'At 6½ dined at Col
Boileau's.' (Lang was a friend of the Boileau sons.) 'Made the acquaintance
of the two Misses Boileau: it seemed the amusement to talk to one another
on our fingers as one Miss B. is deaf and dumb.' He might concentrate
here on the unusual handicap of the younger sister Grace − his family
would all become adept at finger speech − but within weeks he was
denying rumours that he was courting Miss Sarah. By July they were
engaged.

yesterday evening I told my love to Sarah Boileau, and she told hers in return, that Col and Mrs Boileau perfectly approve, but of course nothing more has yet been done.

You, of course, dearest Mother, do not oppose the match: you may be sure that I have not lost my heart to anyone whom you would not like to have as a daughter-in-law, and luckily in this case you know somewhat of the family. Of course, I think her perfection of prettiness and goodness: she is rather under than over average height. She has black hair and hazel eyes; she is a very good, affectionate little girl, very fond of her brothers and parents; very good and unselfish, very ladylike you may be sure, or I should at once be put off; a very good, plucky and pretty horsewoman; very well informed, tho' not the remotest degree allied to the faintest of blues; fond of music and plays the concertina very nicely; fond of drawing, and draws and paints figures very well; and (tho' I had great doubts of it yesterday morning) I now thoroughly believe she really returns my love ardently, and will be as loving a little wife as I could wish.

I have always admired her since she came here (the last day of last year) and have found out within the last month that I had lost my heart to her, but I would not persuade myself that she had to me; tho' Frank has tried so hard to encourage that I summoned up pluck to propose — and very very happy I was when I had done so. Will you write to her when you get this? She shall write to you by the next mail, and I shall then be able to write more myself, so will now stop on this subject, tho' the only one I care about just now.

We expect 2nd Punjab Infantry in here, in a day or two: they come up from Multan. The Bombay Fusiliers are such queer fellows, to us quite foreigners. They look more slovenly than our swell officers; wear crumpled jackets, no collars, black neckerchiefs, ride absurd tats [ponies], with swords and pistols on the Mall and wonder at mules, and the number of buggies etc.

Now I must close this. I hope you will be happy to hear that I am engaged; if you knew Sarah Boileau you would certainly be so. I can hardly believe my good fortune.

18 July I need not tell you that I am intensely happy. I go over early in the morning to chota hazri [light breakfast] and stay till nine; then I go off to do my work etc. until I get away to go back again and stay (going out for a ride in the evening) till nine when the ladies go to sleep in the barracks.

Sarah (or Pussy as I have rechristened her, as being the name of affection my lips have been used to at home) is a good religious little girl and will I know help to keep me on the true path. She will be 20 on 6 January next; so I am 5 years and 2 months older than her. I don't know when we are to be married, but I think there is no reason because these are times of danger and disturbance that it should be put off; we are thinking of getting another house in the Artillery lines near to Col Boileau's. Just fancy me a married man! I don't know whatever I shall do!

On the 16th we had an alarm rather riling to Pussy and me: we were sitting alone in pleasant converse when she was dragged off to fly to the barracks. I galloped back to my house among the 49th. However, of course, nothing occurred, and in a few hours all was quiet again.

But I have not much time and must give you public news. Every letter from camp breathes disgust, discontent and weariness: the Artillery and Engineers have no zeal in working when the right battery is 1000 yards and the left 1700 yards from the walls. We can't take Delhi, that's the long and the short of it; and we are going to entrench ourselves. All are losing spirit from want of confidence in the generals: General Reed has left the army, sick; Brigadier Wilson rules in his stead: no pleasant post that: each chief in turn rapidly disappears. (Chamberlain led up under the walls; he is too brave and has suffered his arm being shattered by grape and requiring amputation at the shoulder.)

You English people won't believe our danger. We all longed for this mail, expecting to find England really alarmed. The mail is in and they say: 'Some of the 3rd Cavalry have mutinied, and a *few* officers were murdered'!

22 July Sir John Lawrence, Nicholson, General Gowan etc. have been holding council of war here yesterday morning. They are anything but sanguine as to our prospects; they believe in the notion (now rapidly gaining ground) that Sir Hugh Wheeler and his force have been cut up, and doubt if Sir Henry Lawrence can hold out any longer at Lucknow.

Consequent on this council of war, the Punjab is to be almost denuded of its troops to enable our side to hold its own before Delhi. And all this time we read sickening twaddle in the leaders from *Times, Examiner,* etc. where old women write their views on our great supremacy over our conquered subjects, our might never to be endangered, the Hindu element very strong, but no chance of a row as the Mohammedans are on our side (we are really fighting Cross versus Crescent now), and all such trash.

23 July After one short week of happiness poor little Pussy has her first trial, in my receiving orders to join the army at Delhi. Yesterday, when Colonel Macpherson held up a letter as he drove past on the Mall, I knew

51

well what I should read inside. He says I am to go off by mail-cart as soon as ever I can. So I hope to send off my tent, my bed, and a box of clothes etc. by bullock cart today and follow by mail-cart tomorrow. Poor little Sarah and I were discussing the plans of our new house, and how the garden should be, and so on. I couldn't tell her then, but had to tell her this morning.

25 July, On the River Beas Here I am off to the wars — in a great flat-bottomed, square-sterned, high-prowed, wall-sided barge, in company with a howitzer of Bourchier's Light Field Battery. Ahead of me a string of similar boats full of khaki-dressed soldiers: behind me boats full of more guns and horses. Such a row! Officers swearing, niggers shrieking and shouting, horses, camels, men and doolies passing down to the ghats [wharfs].

I had not time to write yesterday as you may suppose, for except for almost four hours finishing up the most necessary bits of office work, and in packing off my property to Col Boileau's, I was with Pussy. Poor girl! When shall I see her dear face again? These are sad days for Ladies in India. I at least have the satisfaction, which I can't disguise from myself, that I am going off to fight like a man instead of sitting at home in inglorious ease. I shall have been at the most memorable siege of Delhi. It is much worse for her: first Charlie marched for Delhi; then Frank; then she thought she had me safe, and I am going. These are sad partings, but we ought to be grateful we have no more serious sorrows to mourn and are all alive.

26 July, Ambala I crossed the Beas all right and got to Jullundur at 10am. Jullundur looks so green and fresh, large trees and rich grass, a relief after our brown sunburnt Mian Mir. At 4pm I started in an express cart, to cross the Sutlej by nightfall.

At Ludhiana it began to rain, but in an oilskin cap and big military cape I did not care. As night wore on I got most intensely sleepy, plunging head first at the imminent risk of breaking my neck or being driven over. The careful coachwain eventually had to put his arm round my waist to keep me on. I then tried sitting at his feet, but when I slept my feet kept being caught in the wheel. I then tried lying down curled up on the back seat. At last I gave up: from 3 a.m. to 5 a.m. I slept like a top on a charpoy put in the middle of the road. I then woke up and pushed on, and at 8 was at this hotel.

The mail-cart starts this evening at any time between 5 and 12, so that I may expect to be in camp any time between 8 a.m. and 3 p.m.: the former I hope will be nearer the mark; anyhow, this time tomorrow I shall hear the regular boom of the guns and mortars.

OFFICER IN MAIL-CART
Lang was not alone in racing to Delhi by mail-cart. This drawing illustrates
what the cart was like — and what Lang was like. This is not surprising.
The original artist, Captain G.F. Atkinson, was a fellow Bengal Engineer.
He was not himself at Delhi; so he depended on his colleagues for
descriptions of their experiences.

Fancy! Your next letter from your son will be from a pukka soldier.
When I have been once or twice under regular fire and seen men
knocked over right and left of me, I shall feel I can say I am a soldier and
no carpet-knight, and I shall not care half so much for volunteering and
such things incompatible with the duties of your married man!

From your affectionate son A.M. Lang,
who tomorrow will be Field Engineer, 'Avenging Army',
Camp before Delhi, the doomed city of the Moghuls.

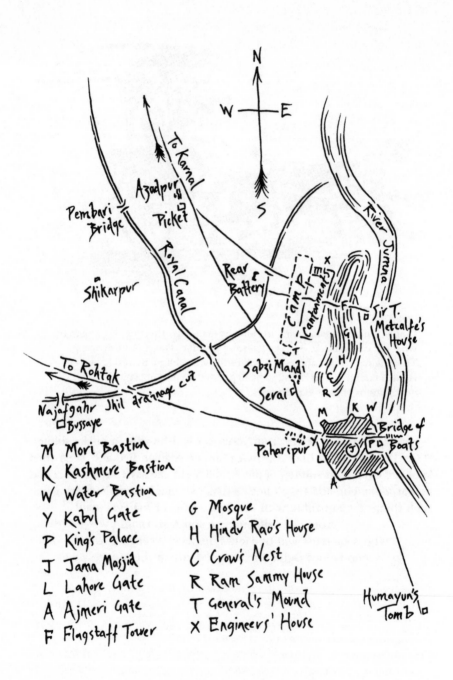

The following labels appear on the map:

To Karnal
Azadpur Picket
Pembari Bridge
Royal Canal
Shikarpur
Rear Battery
River Jumna
Camp (Cantonments)
Sir T. Metcalfe's House
To Rohtak
Najafgahr Jhil drainage cut
Bussaye
Sabzi Mandi
Serai
Paharipur
Bridge of Boats
Humayun's Tomb

M Mori Bastion
K Kashmere Bastion
W Water Bastion
Y Kabul Gate
P King's Palace
J Jama Masjid
L Lahore Gate
A Ajmeri Gate
F Flagstaff Tower

G Mosque
H Hindu Rao's House
C Crow's Nest
R Ram Sammy House
T General's Mound
X Engineers' House

THE BRITISH AT DELHI, JULY 1857

54

CHAPTER 4

Besieged

Lang joined the British army on the Ridge outside Delhi on 27 July. Under the uninspiring, but well-organized, command of Brigadier Wilson (its fourth leader in as many months) the Delhi Field Force was not so much besieging as besieged. A remarkable change, however, was on the way.

Lieutenant-Colonel Baird Smith had just taken charge of the small group of Engineer officers. For the moment they were engaged in a defensive role: that of strengthening the British defences and trying to knock holes in the bridge of boats across the Jumna by floating rafts of explosives downstream. However, inspired by Baird Smith and the energetic Captain Alex Taylor, they were about to play the key role in the eventual storming of the city. Meanwhile, the untrained sweepers they would have to train to be sappers and pioneers for the assault were on the way from the Punjab.

The Delhi Field Force was an extraordinarily polyglot affair. As with any 'British' force in India, the great majority of the troops were not from Britain but from the sub-continent. Of course only a handful were Hindu and Moslem troops (Of this handful many were Bengal Sappers, not all of whom had mutinied: Lang sometimes refers to these trained troops with some relief as 'true sappers'.). There were, however, thousands of Gurkhas, Punjabis and Afghans, attracted by hope of plunder and the promise of revenge on their traditional enemies, the 'Poorbyas' of Bengal.

The officers of the mutinous Native Regiments now found themselves raising and commanding new Irregular regiments. The dashing cavalry commander, Captain Hodson, had himself raised a new regiment, Hodson's Horse (the Plungers). The Guides, his former corps of fiercely loyal Sikhs and Gurkhas, were also in camp. Of even more significance, the charismatic Brigadier Nicholson was on his way, with the Movable Column from the Punjab. Not far behind him too was a siege-train from Firozpur, with elephants, camels and 700 carts, bringing the guns they would need for the assault. The tide was about to turn.

28 July, The Camp before Delhi Here I am in camp, actually with the Army before Delhi, and here I have been for upwards of 24 hours. I have visited most parts of the camp, spied into Delhi from all sorts of positions, and feel I know all about it. I have had round shot and shell pass me, tho' at respectable distances, and have the gratification of having had a shrapnel shell burst close and pour its shower of bullets round me. Altogether I am very jolly.

First to say where I am, and then to resume the thread of events. I am in one of the only houses remaining in Delhi cantonments. The cantonments are a mass of jungly compounds with skeletons of houses, but this is a pukka house, which Engineer officers have seized: the three main rooms are the bedroom, the mess room, the Chief Engineer's office. There are 21 officers of the corps here:

Col Baird Smith — Chief Engineer
Capt Taylor — Commanding Right Attack
Lt Greathed — Commanding Centre Left Attack
Lt Chesney — Brigade Major of Engineers
Lt Gulliver — Commanding Punjab Sappers
Lt Maunsell — Commanding Sappers and Miners
Lt Salkeld — In charge of Engineer park [equipment store]

Field Engineers. Lts Stewart, Warrand, Brownlow (Elliot Brownlow's brother) Geneste, Lang, Thomason. 2nd Lt Champain. Asst Field Engineers. 2nd Lts McNeil, Tandy, Ward, Fulford, Carnegie, Thackeray, Forbes.

Although the smell from the carcases of camels, horses and Pandies [sepoy mutineers] is most offensive, the camp looks exceptionally pretty, the lines of white tents, beyond the green swampy meadows, stretching along the foot of the 'Ridge', which is a long line of hill ground covered with grass, low trees and boulders, on which stand conspicuously the various points: the Flagstaff Tower, the Mosque, Hindu Rao's house — all of which are now posts of our Army: the former with Infantry and Horse Artillery (2 light guns on the road); the second with Infantry and Artillery (heavy battery in front); the third with Infantry and lots of batteries about it. The last is the home of the Sirmaur battalion, from which the Gurkhas I expect are never to go until exterminated.

Yesterday afternoon Geneste, McNeil and I drove out in Brownlow's dogcart to the top of the Ridge (which hides our camp from Delhi), and from the top of the Flagstaff battery had really the most lovely view: anywhere you could call it lovely, but to a man fresh from the level, brown Punjab, it was doubly so. We looked out towards Delhi, a most picturesque city, the red walls and fine gateways of the Palace, the splendid Jama Masjid mosque, the red walls with the bastions, now so well known to us all (the Water, Kashmere, Mori, all on the north front, are our enemies); the broad Jumna with its green banks; the bridge of boats with crowds of Pandies passing and re-passing – altogether a beautiful and most interesting view. The evening was cool and bright, the atmosphere intensely clear after the rain, all the country, undulating hill, covered with trees, fresh and green.

We drove along the top of the Ridge to the Mosque, from the roof of which we had if anything a prettier view and clearer, because nearer. We could see the Mori Bastion well knocked to pieces, but they are making a retrenchment in it; we could see too the Lahore and Kabul Gates; from the latter and the next (the Ajmeri) the enemy march out by regiments to the attack, on a beautiful park-like plain: too much covered with trees to enable one to see well.

It being dangerous to drive further along the Ridge, we drove home and then McNeil and I rode out again, only the inner (our) foot of the Ridge to our extreme right; we rode thro' the 'Valley of Death' all indented with shells and the trees torn with shot, but none passed thro' till we just got out of it. We went to the Sabzi Mandi picket. The S.M. is a suburb of Delhi behind the Ridge and we have our advanced picket on the right there. We dismounted and climbed the Ridge to the 'Crow's Nest', a battery of little Coehorn mortars, and still higher to our right battery. Shrapnel and shot passed about there frequently. One shrapnel shell burst rattled on the stones around us.

30 July Yesterday Charlie Boileau came over and had a chat with me. It was a dull rainy afternoon but we strolled up to the Flagstaff Tower. At 5 pm Greathed and I, Warrand and Brownlow, rode to the left of the position and studied the various streams of the river, relative to devices for smashing the bridge.

At 2 this morning I was up and went over to the Engineer park, got my proper number of pioneers, carpenters, ten elephants, and implements of sorts and marched off to Metcalfe's picket – Sir T. Metcalfe's ruined house. Peacocks swarm there. The house itself is not held, but a very fine set of stables in advance of it form a first-rate post.

I got a covering party of the 1st Fusiliers and posting them as a line of sentries about a quarter of a mile beyond our post, I proceeded to construct an abattis [tree entanglement], cutting down big trees, and making the elephants drag them into position; as day came on, Pandies, skulking in the thick jungly gardens beyond, fired some shell and round shot very well at the elephants: one round came so close as I was working on an elephant amongst a lot more that I quite thought it was on us; only just over us it was. We got home about 11 to breakfast. There's my first day's duty.

31 July One of our officers has just come in to say that the Pandies have marched out in force − guns, cavalry and infantry − and have made a wide detour to the west; some of our troops have gone out to the rear; the enemy are probably after the Kumaon battalion, and the convoys which they must be bringing in today. I must go and see if I can learn more about it. I am on duty from 5 o'clock this afternoon for 24 hours as field engineer on the right battery, Sabzi Mandi etc. As they are banging away hard today, I expect I shall have lots to do and be well tired out. I was sent off last night to the only bridge we have left within ten miles of this on the canal to blow it up in case the enemy come at it.

4 August Four days have passed without my writing a line to you, but really it is not easy work to write. Every day of course I have to write a letter to my little lady love in Lahore Citadel, because a day missed in the daily post of this country is like a letter missed in my half-monthly post to you. The H.Q. of the Artillery Division, consisting I only fancy now of Col Boileau (commanding), Lt Watson (Adjutant) and no men, were ordered down to Lahore Citadel. Of this I am very glad for the very day after they had gone into the Citadel, what should you think happened? The favourite and most trusted of the Mian Mir regiments, the 26th Light Infantry, after having waited nearly three months quiet, disarmed as they were, mutinied!

They were commanded by Major Spencer, a man never hardly seen in society, caring little for European companions, very 'native' in his habits and predilections, loving his regiment among whom he had spent his life. This man had felt more keenly than his men the disarming of his regiment, and had hardly held up his head since: yet these ungrateful, brutal fiends murdered and hacked to pieces with hatchets this officer, who cared for them more than anything else: oh what hateful wretches they are! They searched every officer's house, not to loot but to murder, but poor Spencer, the sergeant major, and some native officers alone lost their lives. The 26th made a dash at the Punjab battalion camp to seize arms; the Sikhs resisted and killed some. The Artillery and 81st were ordered out to pursue by Brigadier Corbett, and nine men caught alive were instantly blown away from guns.

I hear that Gowan stopped the pursuit. I hope it is true that he is going to be sent away on sick leave! So we get rid of incompetent fools in a crisis. All the villages turned out and hunted the 26th like wild beasts, and 400 were killed the first day. When I heard today, only fifty men were alive; by this time they may have shared the fate of their brothers. So may every N.I. regiment disappear, hopes everyone.

We hear that Havelock defeated the Nana Sahib and dispersed his force. He was the brute that massacred the Cawnpore people. At Bithur the troops came across bodies of women and children lying murdered and mangled. The men broke their ranks and butchered every man, woman and child they saw. The 32nd have a heavy debt to repay: all their women and children were murdered at Cawnpore. I suspect that when Delhi falls the sack of the place will transcend in barbarity any known sack in history. The English soldier once roused is as bloodthirsty as any man in the world, and seldom have they met a foe who merited their hatred as have the Pandies. The rest of our army is composed of as ruthless a set as could be found — Sikhs and Afghans, and the most thoroughly cruel of races, the little kukri-bearing Gurkhas. If I am alive at the assault and survive it I shall take precious good care to get clear out of Delhi when the storming is effected.

Well, now I will tell you what we have been doing in camp since I wrote on 31 July. That afternoon I rode off at 5 p.m. through drenching rain to the Sabzi Mandi Serai picket. Sabzi Mandi is about a mile and more from the walls. We now hold it, having looted it, and we take away woodwork etc. to our park. At the corner nearest Delhi is a large serai [inn]; in this we have a strong European infantry picket; in a temple close by we have another smaller one. These are the 'Serai' and the 'Faqueer Takia' pickets.

The Serai is a large rectangular courtyard with flat-roofed rooms all round it and one gateway entrance: the roofs of these rooms form a fine terraced walk all round, on the outer edge of which are raised parapets of sandbags with little loopholes for musketry. It poured for nearly all my 24 hours of duty from 5 p.m. 31 July to 5 p.m. 1 Aug. At 7 in the evening my party of sappers and pioneers came and, after supplying them with tools and materials, I marched them up the hill to the right battery and set them to work to repair the parapets and do whatever work I thought was necessary. I had a charpoy at the Serai on which I got a little sleep — very 'damp' slumber. During the evening the Pandies brought out a 6-pr gun and tried it on us: their firing was bad and we went out and brought in the only ball which hit the walls.

All the next day the Pandies came out in bodies and fought the right batteries and Serai and their outposts. They never came nearer than between two and three hundred yards of the Serai. Tho' they evidently occasionally meditated a charge, neither the perpetual blowing of the 'Advance' nor the shouts of 'Chalo Bhai' ['Come along, brother'] could get them on. Our picket were 8th King's, armed with Brown Bess: this the Pandies soon found out and treated us with contempt, exposing themselves to us. The Gurkhas and Guides, in the small breastworks on the slope of the hill in front of Crow's Nest and the right battery, fought these Pandies all day.

At one time, for an hour or two, a lot of Guides (khaki, every atom of their clothing) came down on the road between us and the Pandies and fought beautifully. They never throw away a shot and are as cool and fearless as any men I know, lying down like stones on the road, getting quietly up and taking steady aim, then down they lie again. For this fighting they are far superior to Europeans: you will see a little pretence of breastwork, about 2½ or 3 feet high: to be sheltered, the Guides must actually lie down: they won't stir: if a Pandy shows an inch over, he is shot; but the Guide won't show *himself*: a Guide will have his hand on the breastwork on one side, and a Pandy on the other side, but the Guide won't stir. Thus a few Guides will hold an almost untenable position against lots of Pandies all day, whereas the Europeans would have either cleared the Pandies off altogether or have been nearly all killed or driven back: so you would lose a lot of men and probably be often driven in. The Guides, on the contrary, will hold the post, hardly lose a man, and will polish off many a Pandy.

On the evening of the 1st, when I got back to our Engineer house, I found Ski, from whom I knew that the Kumaon battalion, the Artillery ammunition, and Dacres [Dacres Wise, Lang's cousin], with the 4th Lancers' horses, had arrived. Soon Dacres, with a formidable beard, made his appearance, looking very well and jolly: he, Ski, Charlie Boileau and I went up to the Flagstaff to see the fight: the troops were all turning out and Charlie Boileau had to rush off to fall in with the 61st.

The city looked beautiful though the view was an indistinct one; a faint rosy light tingling the white domes of the Jama Masjid, while the lower part of the building was fading away in twilight. Dacres and I soon got under fire, for as a group of some thirty of us had collected below the Flagstaff, Pandy could not resist the shot so temptingly offered. A big round shot came dead straight at us, struck a rock in front and bounded beautifully just over our heads, smashing a compound wall behind us. I had up to this prided myself on not bobbing or flinching, but this time I fairly bolted with all the rest: luckily the shell did not burst or a lot of us would have been killed and wounded.

The fighting began to be more severe then, and all night they fought what was meant to be a night attack. At Sabzi Mandi they were chiefly the Nimach party, who had sacked Agra. Our loss when they drew off, well licked, next morning was 23 killed and wounded. Their loss was about 500 killed and wounded. When they summoned up pluck to charge (which they did occasionally) right up to the batteries, our grape [grapeshot: bags of bullets etc. fired from guns] played prettily among them, and they left 70 bodies in front of one of our batteries. Poor Travers was shot through the head: he leaves a young widow (not married a year) who is at Lahore.

On the 2nd Dacres and I went out for a ride: we went on the roof of the Mosque which we found a dangerous look-out, for the Mori Bastion guns were firing very straight at the corner dome by which we stood. One shell pitched dead straight about thirty yards short and the fragments flew over our heads. Almost immediately another followed on the same line, pitched only about ten yards off, but did not burst and only covered us with earth and stones. This we thought too much for fun, so descended and rode down to the extreme right of camp, where we have a battery of three 18-pr guns on a fine natural mound called the 'General's Mound'. This being behind the Ridge is only a defensive battery, to close in the right of camp.

When I got home to breakfast I found orders to be off to Azadpur to relieve Warrand. Gulliver lent me a tent, table and chair, Taylor a cook and his paraphernalia, Ski a horse. The greatest discomfort I experience is from not having a single servant — you know how indispensable they are in India. At noon I marched with my sappers, found the Azadpur picket pitched in the most feverish and aguish-looking swamp imaginable, but very jolly compared to the country around which was like a great lake. Here fifty of Hodson's 'Plungers' (as Hodson's new Cavalry Regiment is called) under young Hugh Gough, and the sappers under Warrand, were pitched, a picket so judiciously placed that Pandy might at any time cut them off.

At 4 p.m. Gough and I rode out with two sowars for a reconnaissance down the canal. We rode though water up to our horses' girths to the Pembari bridge, where a charge of powder is lodged ready to be lighted to blow up the bridge as soon as ever the enemy try to cross it. We then rode down the opposite side of the canal to the aqueduct: the canal used to be carried by an aqueduct over the Najafgarh jhil [swamp] cut, so that its waters supplied Delhi and the palace canals, and flowed into the Jumna; but we broke the aqueduct and so from that point to the Jumna you must imagine the canal empty. The other canal is not an irrigation canal, but a drainage one, and carries off the waters of the great Najafgarh jhil: this jhil last year, during the very great rains, covered 150 square miles! The jhil cut protects our rear beautifully.

It was a beautiful evening as we rode down the canal bank and the ride was delightful. We rode on a turf lane; over our heads arched the trees, a beautiful avenue which gives shade all the day, the full canal with its grassy banks flowing along like an English meadow and river. That illusion would be occasionally dispelled as we saw the troops of monkeys cross the path and scampering up the trees, or peacocks strutting proudly along, and parrots flying screaming about, and smelt the strong scent of the babul blossoms; still more so if we looked over our shoulders and at the khaki-coated, crimson-turbanned horsemen at our backs. On coming back we found young Craigie and fifty Guides Cavalry come to relieve Gough and the Plungers. Craigie was two terms below me at Addiscombe. We had Gulliver's tent pitched, and feasted in it and slept.

Next morning Craigie and I rode a long reconnaissance over Pembari bridge, over the swamped country to Shikarpur and on to the Bussaye Bridge. At Shikarpur we bullied the Lumbardar [village headman], got lots of (false, I suppose) information and took a guide to show us the only practicable route (so swamped is the country). We visited the ruins of the Bussaye and Rohtak Road bridges (both of which we have destroyed) and the aqueduct, and rode back by the canal bank as hungry as hunters for breakfast. The enemy didn't appear to shoot at or pursue us at all. In the afternoon we took another reconnaissance by canal banks to the aqueduct and met Charles Gough come out with Guides to relieve Craigie.

Next morning, Gough and I, accompanied by Stewart (relieving me) and Brigadier Grant and Dacres and troopers, went the long round to Bussaye again. After returning and breakfasting at Azadpur I rode back to camp.

6 August Here is the 26 June (English) mail in and yet the mail conveying news of the Delhi and Meerut mutinies is not acknowledged! We are too far from England still and want telegraphs and railways multiplied. Well, it will save families a fortnight of suspense, this delay; we can settle India without the aid of more troops, I hope. My *Home News* made its appearance today but not your letters. I may hope for them tomorrow morning. The last no. of *Little Dorrit*, too, made its appearance, thus completing the set. When Thackeray's new serial commences, please send it out to me. The *Home News* is full of twaddle about the resources of the country of India etc., and we read this with much interest before the walls of Delhi!

Pandy is fighting us today. Three times have the 'Alarm' and 'Assembly' bugles sounded in camp, so I must be off in a minute. Yesterday afternoon I was on duty from 3 till sunset in the mouth of the Najafgarh jhil cut, constructing a heavy raft (of big casks and trees) for the destruction of the bridge of boats: but I am anything but sanguine as to the usefulness of it: there are so many currents and so many shallows and islands and half-sunken trees, that it is a very great chance anything reaching that bridge, however carefully and judiciously it may have been started. We sent two Infernal Machines down yesterday; one struck an island and exploded in fine style; the second, I believe, reached the bridge, but didn't explode.

7 August The enemy were all out yesterday, chiefly on our left front. Their cavalry tried a charge along the road by Metcalfe's ground below the Ridge, but a volley from the Metcalfe picket and a few guns from the Flagstaff and Mosque pickets (at each of which are two light Horse Artillery guns in position) sent them to the right about. Their attack before Ram Sammy House [English slang for an Indian pagoda] was their strongest: there the new Gurkha arrivals were, the Kumaon battalion, of which two officers were hit: one was hit by round shot in the hip, and of course died within an hour; the other, shot in the neck under the ear will probably get over his (musket ball) wound.

The troops were out all night expecting a night attack; the enemy, too, lay out all night and at the first streak of daylight they began again; at least I can answer for the right front on which I have been all the morning. I never saw them keep up such a hot fire of shot and shell on the Sabzi Mandi; they were bursting about us all the time.

8 August By mail-cart yesterday arrived Medley and Hovenden; they join the ranks of the field engineers, a welcome addition. There are now 23 officers of our regiment here.

Our people seem to be beginning to hold their own in Central India now Holkar [The Maharajah of Indore] has remained steadily faithful to us: you may say that these are a few instances of fidelity & that the Hindu and Mohammedan are not utterly bad: the exceptions are so very extraordinarily few, that I insist that all the Mohammedans and Hindus of our presidency are as faithless, cruel and ungrateful race as exist. I certainly think the Mohammedans the worst, but in very many parts of India the Hindus have led the rising and the barharities. I am sure our khits [table servants] and our sappers are in constant communication

63

JOHN NICHOLSON (1822-1857)
Few campaigns have thrown up leaders as charismatic as Brigadier
Nicholson. Though killed in the assault on Delhi, he had by then already
turned the tide. His reputation outlasted the Raj he saved. One hundred
years later when the newly independent Indian government decided to
take down Nicholson's statue in Delhi, not only workmen but a number
of armed men gathered round the statue. Why, asked a British officer, did
they need armed men? The superintendent said, rather sheepishly, that
they feared that Nikal Seyn's spirit might return to punish those who
disturbed his rest.

with the enemy: when the first Infernal Machine was started for the bridge, none knew of the project but Engineer officers and a few sappers; yet on that day not a grasscut [servant who cuts grass for the horses] crossed the bridge to forage. Men evidently waited for these things and knew how to handle them without danger.

The enemy have made a new heavy gun and mortar battery in Paharipur, the suburb outside the Lahore Gate, and it was from that that the heavy firing came into Sabzi Mandi yesterday. A grand explosion in the city caused our men great delight. It was at first supposed that the enemy's magazine had blown up, but there was not noise enough nor was there the appearance of bits of building thrown into the air; it is supposed to have been the explosion of a great quantity of powder laid out to dry.

Last night we made a new battery on the right for heavy mortars to silence this new battery. (Gen. Wilson had the tail of his coat blown away!) A force was to have gone out to take it, but it was thought best first to try and silence it. Nicholson arrived in camp yesterday (alone without his column of troops). I wish he were to have the command of a force to take that battery and I were to be of the party.

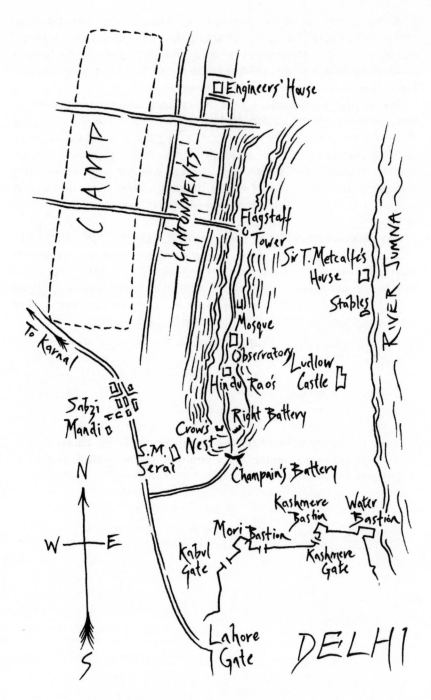

DELHI RIDGE, AUGUST 1857

CHAPTER 5

Fighting Back

Nicholson's arrival marked a turning point in the strategy of the Delhi Field Force, from a concentration on defence towards urgent planning for assault. It also had a profound effect on morale. The British forces recovered their self-confidence, and, far more importantly, the sepoys began to lose their belief in eventual victory.

Despite their vast superiority in numbers, the strength of their defences, the power of their guns and the skill with which they handled them, and the great bravery and even fanaticism with which many of them fought, the mutineers' morale had never been as high as it should have been. The fault lay in their leadership. They had no leaders used to high command, and few who could lead even companies effectively. Now they were to see the enemy force increasing in numbers and firepower, while any efforts they made to cut off its supplies were punished by the brilliant raids of Hodson and Nicholson. They also found their sallies against the forces on the Ridge proving less and less effective.

At this stage in the siege, Lang's role appeared to be little more than one of care and maintenance, though it was care of the most important and maintenance of the most dangerous kind. The Engineer officers had to ensure that the batteries (gun emplacements) on the Ridge were so far as possible protected against gunfire from the city walls. They and their mostly untrained Punjabi sappers had to repair the fortifications behind which the gunners fired.

Compared to the dashing adventures of the cavalry officers it was unglamorous work, but it was to prove invaluable training for what was to be the key operation in the plan of assault.

13 August Four days have passed without me writing you a line. I am still all well and unharmed, I am thankful to say. To be unharmed is always to be a source of wonder, but to be well, tho' we have plenty of exposure here, is not, when one thinks of it, strange. As someone says, 'rust rots the steel use preserves'.

We have too much work, too much to occupy us to allow us to be ill, to let us know when it is hot or wet, or uncomfortable, and we conquer illness it seems generally, for unless the work steeled the mind to forget ills, our bodies ought to suffer at this unhealthy season, in this unhealthiest of localities and amidst this utter recklessness as to precautions and care; but, tho' every one in turn is on the sick list, the general health in camp is capital.

I wrote on the 8th, so, to return to the journal fashion, I will say what I have done each day since. That afternoon I went up for my 24-hour tour of duty to Hindu Rao's house, where the Gurkhas live: mending revetments and embrasures in my batteries was the work. This is a grand three-storied house with a flat roof, from which is a beautiful view of our whole position and of Delhi; but, at the same time, Hindu Rao's is the centre of fire and consequently the roof is no safe look-out.

In the three stories of the house are the sick and wounded of the Gurkhas; at the back of the lower storey are a set of cloisters in which the officers live; at the rear are the stables and outhouses in which the Gurkhas live. In front of Hindu Rao's, looking towards Delhi, is the centre battery; to the left of Hindu Rao's, towards the Mosque, is the Observatory Tower, in front of which is the left battery. Where the Ridge begins to drop towards the right, there Champain's battery crosses and commands it. Of course on all this bit of the Ridge the enemy pour their fire all day and the road running along the top of the Ridge to Champain's battery is a fatal walk when the fire is heavy.

On the 9th I had the worst bit of work I have ever had: carrying platforms from left and centre to Champain's battery, under an exceptionally heavy fire. After three trips Baird Smith and Chesney, escorting Nicholson about the position, came up to the right battery and of course they saw the folly of the order; so I stayed till relief time under the parapet of the right battery.

On the 10th I was again on duty from half past 6 till daybreak, repairing embrasures at the right and Champain's batteries; the moonlight being very bright, the Pandies fired with musketry all night on the parapet and embrasures, but luckily with no manner of effect.

I got three delightful English letters of 19 June. Thanks dearest Mother to you and the dear correspondents. You have heard of me up to 3 May when we were living on out here in a state of rank Pandyism without

LIFE IN THE BATTERIES
For the few heavy guns that had been brought with the Delhi Field Force,
batteries were erected along the Ridge some 1500 yards from the city. The
exhausted gunners fired, as this picture shows, through embrasures
(openings) in epaulments (fortifications) made of fascines (brushwood)
and gabions (wicker baskets filled with earth).

knowing the great convulsions impending. The next letter you will have
received was written under very different circumstances, of martial law,
and station after station was 'going'. What grief and anxiety that mail
must have brought with it into England!

On the 11th I was sleeping during the early part of the day. Dacres
and I rode out in the evening. That night I thought Gustavinski had
cholera and sat up with him a long time; he got alright next day.

On the 12th at about 4 in the morning I heard the steady rattle of
musketry and occasional booming of guns and longed to hear them stop,
that I might imagine our troops had charged in with the bayonet. Soon
Hovenden and Maunsell came in with the most welcome intelligence
that Brigadier Showers's force had taken four guns (two 6-prs, one 9-pr,
one 24-pr). Our loss is 16 killed, 22 wounded. The guns were on the
road just beyond Metcalfe's grounds.

At five I went up to Hindu Rao's. I foolishly went by Valley of Death
road, not knowing what a heavy fire Pandy was keeping up on the centre,
and found it an uncommonly unpleasant ride. Very little work. Two shots
have hit the house just now; one smashed into a room full of wounded
Gurkhas but hit none.

18 August, Hindu Rao's House Here I am again where I was when I last wrote five days ago. This is a hot lazy day and the gunners on both sides seem to have agreed that the sun is too hot to allow of standing out firing guns in the batteries. My work, too, is light. I have only a small party of sappers at work in the centre battery constructing permanent sheds for the Artillery men. I go occasionally to see that all is going well, and very glad I am to return from the glare to the shade of these cloisters, tho' they be tenanted by flies, whose name is legion, and odours of Gurkhas and their dinners. So I have leisure to take up my pen and this letter and narrate the monotony of the days since the 13th. That day eight of my servants and Herat made their appearance.

On the 14th August in marched Nicholson's column: a goodly reinforcement consisting of Her Majesty's 52nd, remaining wing of H.M.'s 61st; the 2nd (Green's) Punjab Infantry, 300 of the 7th Punjab Infantry; 400 Multani Horse, and Bourchier's Light Field Battery. With them came an accession to our party in the shape of Pat Murray and his half-company of sappers, consisting of four Afghans and two Sikhs! The Poorbyas have all been disarmed at Ambala and sent back to the Punjab.

This is a goodly addition to our force. As Sir Henry Lawrence has been told that the army now before Delhi must take it, I hope General Wilson will muster up moral courage enough to order the attack to be commenced in earnest, and that this most unsatisfactory dilly-dallying before Delhi may cease. Pandy is now the attacking and we the attacked party. Pandy holds ground which once was ours: my first piece of duty here was to construct an abattis at the very end of Metcalfe's stables, and now that ground and right up to the stables is held by Pandy, and the stables themselves are nearly untenable − bits of the roof smashed in and many a hole right through the walls. Against our right, too, he advanced, and is getting breastworks run up very near to us at the Pagoda picket and Crow's Nest.

That day the fire was kept up and Taylor's horse was killed by round shot at the Observatory. Greathed, Hovenden and I rode down to the Metcalfe picket in the afternoon and inspected the ground. At 6½ p.m. I went down with a large party of Punjab sappers to spend the night on the trenches and works there: that is a relief I, the sleep-lover, hate.

The 15th was a holiday to me, spent at first in sleep. The 8th band played in camp and I went to listen to the delightful strains of music again. Not much done that day.

The 16th was also a holiday, to my surprise. I never had such a spell − 36 hours clear to myself. I went to see the arrivals in Nicholson's column.

Yesterday Nicholson came to breakfast with Baird Smith. Up I came here and spent the evening on the roof reading. I had a letter from Frank Boileau. He is at Hansi doing nothing, and sighing for Delhi and action.

20 August, Hindu Rao's House Again the same heading; this main picket seems to be coming my own exclusive right; and I have no objections as it is our pleasant post. After writing the other day, I was relieved at 5; then I rode to an auction of poor Travers's property, to try and get a revolver, but did not, as the two for sale were not good ones. It is unfortunate that I should have lent my revolver to Elliot Brownlow, as he has had no occasion to use it, while now revolvers in the plains are not to be had. Men refuse to sell theirs for 500 rupees.

Yesterday I found myself again down for duty at 5 p.m. and consequently came up here. Hodson sent in from within four miles of Rohtak to say that if some troops would come out to him they would take Rohtak and cut up a lot of the enemy. So Nicholson went out last night with six 6-pr guns and 1,200 men towards Rohtak. Charlie Boileau, with some of the 61st, is with him — lucky fellow! A jolly change from camp life, with the pleasure of expecting to meet the enemy.

I forget whether I told you that Dacres was now with the Plungers and had gone out with Hodson on a reconnoitring expedition on the evening of the 14th, not knowing how long he was likely to be out. I have not heard from him since, nor do I expect to, as they go 'daur-ing' [raiding] about in all directions: much better fun for him than sticking in camp, where cavalry have nothing to do.

Last night a battery was made to the left of the Metcalfe stables and two 9-pr guns opened fire from it this morning at dawn to dislodge the enemy's picket, close to the stables: of course all the enemy's guns opened on the new battery and these batteries opened to keep down the enemy, so there was hard cannonading till 9 o'clock, when all stopped. I believe our guns drove the enemy out, on which Infantry advanced and dismantled the building: that will, just for the time, make the stables a more comfortable abode.

22 August The enemy have made a new battery on the opposite side of the river, nearly opposite Metcalfe's house, from which they pitch shell and rockets at the Metcalfe picket, and last night they sent a rocket over and beyond this house: their 'attack' progresses well.

Nicholson's column of 1,200 men, which went out on the night of the 19th, was in camp again at 10 o'clock the next morning: they marched out ten miles to Alipur and, after two hours' halt, marched back again. A letter came in on the night of the 19th from Hodson that he was all serene, had passed Rohtak and was bound northwards. There is no other camp news, except that Home came in yesterday with two more companies of Mazbis, and that Wilson has been made major-general. The siege-train ought to be at Ambala today.

We are going on very monotonously here. I am again in main picket. I have no objection at all: and I believe it is intentional now, as Taylor objects to officers taking not sufficient interest in their work if they don't see it again for days, and this is, of course, the case when an officer is at Hindu Rao's one tour, at Metcalfe's the next, then at Pagoda, then at right battery. There is no camp news.

Shaves [rumours] by the dozen there are, which inventive minds pour upon the camp. One of the last is that the King of Delhi has sent an indignant letter out to know why his last three months' salary has not yet been paid up!

25 August Here we are going on the same as ever, very little being done. Nicholson went out with a force this morning, as the enemy had a large army in the field which went out of Delhi in the direction of Najafgarh jhil. Their object is not known. Perhaps they mean to make a large detour and come on to the Karnal road to seize our siege-train. That would be their last chance: once let us have the siege-train and their day is over. I was in hope that I might get out with this force and get a little change, and thinking I was next on roster duty was beginning to make arrangements last night, but Geneste's was the next tour of duty, so off he was sent.

Hodson's force came in yesterday morning; he and his 300 sowars returned with no men killed, and only one officer and 14 men wounded, and had killed 88 of the enemy's sowars. They had two fights, one on foot in a village, and another before the walls of Rohtak, a cavalry engagement. The Guides and new Plungers fought capitally. At the village seven desperate men got into a house, and held it, firing pistols and carbines out of the door and our men firing theirs in; the dodge of burning grass being tried, out rushed the seven. Hugh Gough caught the slash of no. 1 on his sword but slipped and fell backwards: Charles Gough rushed forward and put his sword through no. 1 as he was going to kill Hugh and with a backstroke cut down no. 2; nos. 3 and 4 rushed on Ward who, with one ball, killed no. 3, and, as that party fell on him, he shot no. 4 over his shoulder. Hodson cut another down and the Guides two more; all this done in a second or two must have been stirring fun. Dacres standing within a yard of the door (before they came out) was struck by bits of brick and mortar sent flying by a ball fired at him from within.

The force at Hisar was attacked by 4,000 of the enemy: after the firing

CAMELS TAKING TROOPS TO DELHI
Troops hurrying to Delhi were mounted in the camel panniers in which
the cooking materials were usually carried. In these they could cover some
forty miles a day, instead of the usual twelve or fifteen. Lang points out
that animal transport was used later for the European troops racing to
Agra, but that the Punjabi troops marched there.

from the walls had disposed the enemy to give in, the gates were thrown
open and Frank Boileau with the Cavalry charged out; his men didn't
back him up well, but on he charged far ahead and by his dashing charge
turned the enemy, and his men eventually came up; he tried to capture
one sowar himself and would not let his men help: consequently one
cut on the wrist disabled him; his enemy gave him a fearful slash over
cheek and jaw, severing the bone. The loss of blood was very great, and
the wound very difficult to clean and close; however, it is now bound
up and poor Frank fed by means of a quill; so on liquids he will be for
a long time fed, poor fellow. God grant he may get over this very severe
wound.

The English mail was in at Bombay on the 5th: it tells us of great
excitement in England and the vast preparations to send *at once 4* !!!!!
regiments by the Cape!!! to help the authorities to quell the disturbance
and says no one can deny that our govt is taking most prompt and
energetic measures! By Jove, I vote as soon as we have licked Pandy on

our own account to defy that energetic prompt govt to turn us out of India: the fools! and to send of all men Sir Colin Campbell out! He knows nothing of Indian requirements and hates the EIC army. Sir Pat Grant is the best man for the work.

My daily news is as usual; 22nd-23rd on main picket; 24th and 25th I have been in camp; tonight I suppose it will be main picket again. We have very heavy rain today. I hope it will again drive cholera out of camp. Tennant arrived this morning to make our 26th Engineer officer here. I had some shot-putting with artillery men.

26 August Having to go off in another hour's time to the ground in front of our new trench and stay out till dusk, cutting down trees etc., which afford Pandy cover, I have come in from the batteries to write a bit to you, as I believe I ought to send off my letter tomorrow. Nicholson came across the enemy yesterday afternoon at 4½ p.m. and administered a good thrashing at Najafgarh, taking twelve guns, and dispersing them in all directions. He took so many tumbrils [carriages] that he could not bring them all in and (hang it, there is the alarm again) had to blow a lot up. Consequently Pandy is excessively riled and has been pounding from Water, Kashmere and Mori Bastions at us and making his absurd charges to within 150 yards of the batteries. Nearer he will not come, but keeps 'pinging' away into our batteries from the low walls at that distance. I have been out watching the fun for the last half hour or so. Our riflemen and doses of grape had, I thought, quieted them, but the alarm has sounded again, and swords again are buckled on and out I shall go again. Pandy has brought out six more guns and his cavalry are pouring out, so I suppose he has summoned up pluck for an attack: his courage will fail him before he has done much. I expect the place where I was to cut down trees will be for an hour or two inhabited by Pandies and much traversed by balls from our Guides and Gurkhas in the trench . . . .

I got tired of the sun in the batteries and have come in. Pandy is a coward: he has been and is going on with his fusilade and cannonade and we reply, but he won't charge right up. Our grape has sent many of them off, carried away, dead or wounded, and of course every now and then we get a man hit: one rifleman just now came in, shot thro' the leg, not caring for the wound, but anathematizing his luck to have been engaged twenty-three times and at last to be hit by one of his own side. Another fellow has just come in, with a jolly hole in his forehead, but luckily he was hit sideways and the ball has gone out again. This poor shattered house has had one or two bad raps today. My tree-cutting party is knocked on the head.

I had a warm affectionate letter from Elliot Brownlow congratulating me on my engagement: he confesses to a first feeling of being stunned at the fall of all our *Chateaux en Espagne:* our trips to England together, travels in Italy, Alps, Pyrenees, Norway, our enjoyment together again of Opera, Epsom, Ascot, and Goodwood, Chiswick — all these plans done for. But he now says he builds new castles for himself and me and he means to be an intimate friend and guest of AML the married just as he would have been of his bachelor friend. He is such a fine fellow. I wish you knew him. Such a manly, courageous, energetic happy fellow, and now grown so earnest and straightforward a Xtian! He wrote still thinking I was at Lahore, and sent little Miss Sarah a letter. He hopes to come down to the plains at the end of October, when he hoped he might give *me* away. I dare say he and I shall be fighting side by side next November instead of being principal and assistant at weddings.

27 August Your letters of the 3rd July reached me today. Little did you think that your letters would find me on service before Delhi, yet untaken! Most of your questions and surmises will have been settled before now. I did for a short time believe in our Mian Mir regiments: how falsely. As you say, had it not been for Mr Montgomery's and Brig Corbett's promptness (under God), Lahore would have been the Delhi of the Punjab.

Very, very grateful ought I to be that I have yet been spared by God's mercy till now thro' all these dangers, and God grant that I may feel it more and really from my heart how powerless I am and how petty is this world and all my earthly hopes and plans and how in our Saviour alone and in His service can true dependence and happiness be found: but how very hard and thankless our natural hearts are.

Goodbye Dearest Mother for another mail, and God grant that the next mail may relieve your anxiety by telling you of the fall of Delhi and of my safety and security in India. Best love to all the very loved home circle.

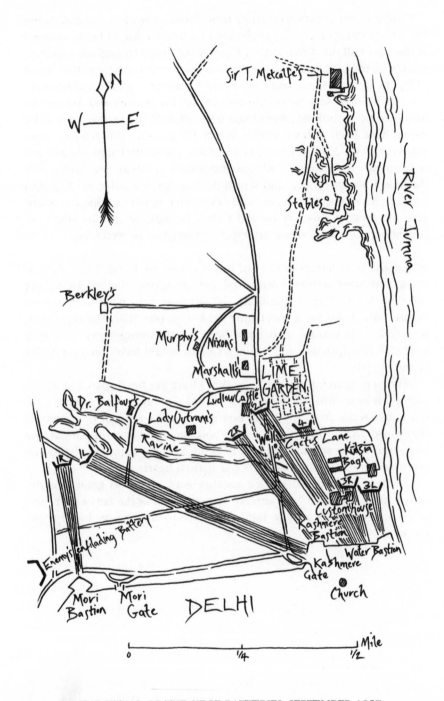

THE SITING OF THE SIEGE BATTERIES, SEPTEMBER 1857

CHAPTER 6

Preparing The Assault

At the start of September the siege-train with its big guns arrived, and the plan of attack could at last be put into operation. This plan has been attributed variously, either to Baird Smith or to Taylor. Most historians give Baird Smith the credit. Most of the Engineer officers thought Taylor should have had it, and John Nicholson himself said: 'If I live, I will let the world know who took Delhi .... that Alexander Taylor did it.' The confusion was largely due to the extraordinary secrecy that surrounded the preparations.

The plan necessitated the building of batteries close enough to the walls for the big new guns to smash major breaches through which the troops could storm the city. The problem was that the batteries would have to be built within close range of the Pandies' guns; and so great would be the counter-bombardment that the breaches would have to be made within a day or so.

The Ridge itself was far too far away for its batteries to do the work. The ideal site lay between a house called Ludlow Castle and the Kashmere and Water Bastions. Here there was a ravine which would give the sappers some protection as they brought what would be a huge convoy of materials from the Ridge to the sites of the siege batteries. Amazingly the enemy had allowed this area to remain part of no-man's-land. They neither occupied it nor left pickets there. They seemed to expect a frontal assault in the area of the Lahore Gate.

The Engineers' plan was first to establish a battery to knock out the guns of the Mori Bastion, and then to establish three siege batteries (one of them only 160 yards from the walls) in front of Ludlow Castle. These would make the breaches. We may never know for certain who devised the plan, but there is no doubt that it was Taylor who carried it out. He reconnoitred exactly where he wanted each gun placed, and Nicholson himself accompanied him. Not even Taylor's own officers knew these locations until he sent them out to build the batteries. Meanwhile they were to concentrate on training their sappers on battery-building, and the assault troops on escalading [placing and climbing ladders in an assault].

When they did receive their orders from Taylor, they found he had committed them to something that had never been achieved before. No 1 battery would have to be built within one night, and preparation for the three siege batteries was to be carried out at the same time. It would take superb teamwork to combine the operations, but Taylor thought his officers could do it − and they proved him right.

29 August, Camp Delhi I sent off a letter to you on the 27th. Very many thanks I again send to you, Pussy and Aunt Mary, for your respective letters. I wish that communication between us could be quicker. It is, as you say, in these times that one feels how distant India really is. I am glad that, although you are naturally very anxious, you consoled yourself by supposing that the worst was over and that no more regiments would rise. How mistaken a notion when they still are rising. Why, this very mail will tell you of the worst massacre of all (the Cawnpore one) and of the state of Lucknow (still unrelieved) and of Delhi still supporting the green standard. And our fools of rulers at home prate in the House of Commons of the ease with which Delhi, a city with a circuit of seven miles and with eleven gates, can be surrounded and taken. They deserve to lose India. However coolly they take it, where would England be without India, a third-rate power, wealth and prestige lost? I consider our position just now more dangerous than it has been for a couple of months past.

The siege-train has not yet crossed the Markanda. When will it arrive? I was on duty yesterday from 3½ a.m. till noon, working at the new battery, on which the enemy kept up a steady shower of shot, shell and grape, firing excessively well: but the sun was the most trying enemy. I suppose that, tho' rain is stopping, we shall have a great deal of fever. Cholera is again carrying off great numbers, especially in the 52nd and 61st. This long delay will have cost us many more lives than an assault.

31 August I wrote the day before yesterday, Saturday the 29th. After mess that evening, just as I was going off to bed, I received orders (as did three others) to go down at once and reinforce Warrand's party of

ELEPHANTS IN SIEGE-TRAIN
In the Mutiny all the heavy work was done by animals. The siege-train, the
key to the assault on Delhi, extended some seven miles and depended
entirely on bullocks and elephants. Pulling and pushing 'with remarkable
sagacity', the elephants brought nearly fifty pieces of heavy ordnance,
together with innumerable carts of ammunition, from Ambala to Delhi.

four officers and 300 sappers, who were out in front of our right, clearing
away the jungle to within three or four hundred yards of the walls. The
enemy were charged out of their line of breastworks opposite our right
front (which only cost one rifleman killed and two wounded) and then
our covering parties of Rifles, Guides and Gurkhas used their breastwork
and held it, and 300 sappers with felling axes were launched into a
square mile or more of seven-foot grass jungle to cut down the trees.

Axes were soon ringing away in all directions and musketry rattling
away along our front and the bullets flying through the jungle. At first,
wading about this jungle and prying out Pandy's haunts, his walls, and
hollows and rifle pits, so to speak, and the paths, well worn, leading to
them, and to come out of the edge of the jungle and look over the clear
narrow plain at the near walls and listen to Pandy's alarm and assembly
bugles as they rang through the city, warning the Mata Deens [sepoys]
to be on the alert against what they took to be an assault on the city –
all this at first, when clear bright moonlight shone over all the scene,
was very exciting, novel and pleasant, but when at twelve the moon
went down and all was dark and the sappers (the new Punjab, raw,

undisciplined dogs), trusting to the dark, the thick cover, and the scattered position, took to skulking from bullets and work, by hiding in the grass, and when to keep them at work necessitated perpetual fruitless wandering through the 'pathless wilds,' tumbling into crevices and pits and over ruined walls — the work ceased to be jolly.

At about 3½ a.m. Warrand told me to collect all and go to a certain point, that we might as a last measure destroy the breastworks which our covering parties were holding. With great trouble we got together eight officers and about 300 men and off we waded single file, through the ocean of high grass, six officers leading and two whipping in: arrived at a sandy lane, our rendezvous, then called out for all the men to lie down, as Pandy was quite close and his bullets flying fast.

At last up came Warrand growling and wondering what had become of his party. I hailed him and said, 'Here we are 8 officers and 300 men.' 'All right then, up you get.' Up we got, and found that six officers and eleven men was our party! It was absurd! The rest had quietly, somewhere in the jungle, broken off single file and gone off where we didn't know; eventually they were found at the Pagoda picket and the two whippers-in wondering where they had whipped in their men! After futile attempts to get our men, we all came back and drew in the covering parties as day was coming on.

We lay then on that path under bullets, so merry, and chaffing poor Warrand on his futile plans, and the next we saw of him was that evening, brought in with his arm shattered dreadfully by shell. He and a sapper were doing something to the embrasure in the new Pagoda battery and a shell bursting in the embrasure smashed W's left and the sapper's right arms. In the same battery one sapper had been killed and another lost his arm that day, too, and today some five or six have been hit: now that it is nearly finished it is more dangerous, apparently, than it was when but commenced and when there was hardly any shelter.

I have been sitting all day by poor Warrand's bedside. His left arm was amputated at the shoulder last night under chloroform: it is sad to see so fine, tall, broad-shouldered a fellow lying there with his whole arm gone and weak and helpless. It is these scenes and results which make war sad: before the enemy we laugh and think nothing of danger or misery and suddenly down goes some friend and then one feels that it is no pleasant exciting pastime, this war, but a fatal reality.

Yesterday afternoon I went to the Cavalry camp where service was held in the open air. A Rev. Rotton officiated: his sermon was not very impressive — his object to urge the men to spare women and children in the storm.

Charlie Boileau has joined the Foot Artillery as a volunteer officer in the centre battery. This morning he showed me a letter from a comrade of Frank's at Hansi, and a copy of a note which Frank had written on a slate. Frank bore the removal from Hisar to Hansi very well.

I am glad I am not on duty tonight; it is pelting hard; the rains must soon break up; then heigh for fevers. I said casually at mess that we would have 'theatricals' in the Jama Masjid, and Baird Smith said 'Oh! you won't be three days in Delhi before you all go off to new fields.' I hope that is true.

2 September No news particular in camp. There is a quiet lull before the storm, which must break when the siege-train comes in. I am for the present taken off the regular duty roster and have daily to instruct the troops (European infantry) in escalading. Last night I was out for instruction in platform-laying; it is a great bore having to instruct all these raw Sikh recruits in the duties of sappers; however fine a corps the Punjab Sappers may be some day, they are undisciplined, stupid recruits now, and a sapper can't be formed under a couple of years. We feel now the great loss of 1,000 well-trained sappers. These fellows make such a row, and know nothing of what they have to do.

4 September The siege-train is here at last. Hurrah for that: now we may begin in real earnest. I have been out this morning to see our new heavy guns in the Artillery park: 22 there are: four 10″ mortars, four 8″ howitzers, six 24-pounder guns, and eight 18-pounder guns, a goodly show, cheering the spirits. Now, Mr Pandy, you may as well shut up!

The Beluchis, too, have come in, such strange wild-looking fellows: bright dark green, laced with red, red caps with green turbans. I hope they are plucky and ferocious.

Now our work must begin in good earnest and I am happy to say that I am all well again and shall be fit for hard work. I have never been on the sick-list but I was at one time nearly going on, and put myself in the doctor's hands, when, luckily, I made a start the right way and became well again: once getting seedy in this camp, one generally gets worse and then to rally is very hard work.

On the evening of the 2nd Dacres paid me a visit and we strolled in the headquarter camp and listened to the band. I dined last night with him at his new Plunger mess. Hodson himself dined there. Hodson stayed with you once for some time at Allahabad.

Yesterday morning I was up at 4½ a.m. instructing some of the 8th and 61st in escalading. I shall have some more escalading this afternoon. The European soldiers and their officers hate the thought of escalading.

I hope the men won't be the less ready to mount for this, or else it will be all up with 'us poor critturs as leads'.

Col Baird Smith is seated in conclave in the next room with Gen Wilson, Nicholson, and Major Hogge, the Commissary of Ordnance, and I suppose they are setting our fate for us. On the 1st we received one addition, Pemberton, making No. 27 in the list of Engineer officers, but our corps is short-handed with so many of our officers falling sick.

I wish there were more of us, for as it is it seems most probable that the first night of battery making will expend half of us, and the assault the survivors. It will be a sad day, that of the assault, for tho' everyone who survives must exult in heart when all is over, yet how sad will be our next meeting to mess. So very heavy must be the loss our unfortunate corps must sustain, and we all know one another as friends, who are under fire daily together, and meeting altogether every day at a time when all must feel drawn to one another.

I mean to make my will now in favour of Dacres, who will not be exposed during the next week as we shall be. He will take charge of my things, and prevent everything I have here being rummaged about and sold by auction. I should hate all my traps put up for sale, before at least some friend had weeded out a good many articles.

6 September Last night a quiet commencement of the work was made by Thackeray, who with a lot of pioneers occupied a natural ravine which runs about three or four hundred yards from the walls: in this he worked at filling sandbags, all ready for the batteries. I expect that tonight nearly all our officers will be out on the work, clearing the ground, and tomorrow night will be commenced the batteries.

I continue my escalade drilling morning and evening and consequently have pleasant regular work and keep well. Sickness is on the increase. The 61st alone have lost two officers and sixty men of cholera in ten days, and so the sooner the assault is given the better. Warrand is getting on very well. I sat with him for a long time yesterday and wrote letters for him.

This morning a reinforcement from Meerut came in, 200 riflemen and 100 Artillery recruits. No more are to come, except Wilde's Corps and Maharajah Ranbir Singh's contingent, but we can do without these, and they will be up in time to guard camp while we go in for the assault. We have been sharpening our swords, kukris and dirks, and tried cutting silk handkerchiefs after breakfast: my 'favourite fighting sword' Excalibur, one of Aunt Mary's presents, has now an edge like a razor and a surface like a mirror.

9 September I will write you a few lines to be despatched by tomorrow's dak, so as to ensure you a bit of news of me by the Marseilles mail. We are now in the very thick of it, salvoes roaring away all day, and we unlucky Engineer officers fagging away hard.

We opened the attack at 6 p.m. on the 7th, when our covering parties under Col Greathed of the 8th, with Greathed and Murray of our corps, advanced up the road to the Kashmere Gate and without opposition occupied a line from the Kudsia Bagh on the left to a point below the Ridge on the right, about 550 yards from the Mori Bastion; this line and all in rear was occupied. Then down came the working parties, some 3,000 men, Europeans and Natives, under about ten or twelve Engineer officers: strings of camels carrying empty sandbags poured down the road and the appearance was as of two or three regiments marching.

Pandy most strangely shut up and we did what we liked opposite a city that appeared deserted. What Pandy meant by it we can't imagine; he must have thought himself a precious fool when battery no. 1 right, and no. 1 left, opened, the one with six and the other with four heavy guns, at dawn of day on the Mori Bastion. It was *very, very* creditable work; those two batteries, composed of fascines and sandbags, were constructed in one night, magazines made and platforms laid, the guns brought − all by daybreak. No. 1 right and left opened and the Mori fought them. My friends Salwey & Charlie Boileau are both in no. 1 right, not to return till Delhi has fallen. Poor Hildebrand, one of our Mian Mir Artillery officers, had his head knocked off by a round shot: a good many Rifles and Artillery men were hit during the first half-hour after dawn, but then the old Ridge batteries banged away to the rescue.

I had 100 of the 8th who were employed in filling sandbags for battery no. 2 left, and 100 of the 61st, sandbags for battery no. 2 right: 100 Sikhs and 70 Gurkhas for filling sandbags and making a traverse across the road by the upper gate of Ludlow grounds. From 6 p.m. till 5 a.m. I never sat down and I don't remember when I was ever before so tired, going about to my three different parties, urging them on, building sandbags up with my own hands.

On 8 September, when I woke at 12 I found a note to tell me to be on duty at 1½ p.m. After a hasty breakfast, off I started again with 100 Beluchis and 80 Wilde's Punjabis: they worked in the two places as last night. The fire was very heavy indeed. From Cactus Lane to the lower gate of the Ludlow grounds bullets and grape were dancing about the road, and I taking Beluchis (one at a time) down that road had to make the trip at least forty times. They funked so that they would rush into the hedge and lie down and drop their pickaxes and spades. I would stand in the middle of the road and pelt them with stones and shout at them, and make rushes at them and kick them up and drag them along, the curs. Only two were hit. At last I got them in that hollow, and left them with a sergeant to work.

I then went to the Punjabis near the well in front of Cactus Lane, and set them to work. An hour later I went back to my Beluchis. They had now turned against my mild young Sapper sergeant and, keeping under cover, refused to work. I rushed like a shell amongst them, knocked about a dozen down, kicked as many more and swore I would hang the first who hesitated for an instant to obey me. The effect was splendid: they obeyed me in grand fear, while I walked up and down and likened them to trembling women. At 7 p.m. we stopped and marched back. I had the pleasure of a night in bed.

10 September Yesterday no. 4, a mortar battery in Sir T. Metcalfe's garden, was made out and at daybreak was armed with ten mortars. During the night no. 2 right and left were half made. I was up at 10 expecting to be on duty. Dacres paid me a visit. At 5 I was at duty under Medley at no. 2 right, and worked away hard until about 6 a.m. We finished three platforms and two magazines and made the battery shotproof. Before daybreak the guns (five 8″ howitzers and two 18-pr guns) were brought into battery.

It was so hot that I was up and dressed by 10. At 1 p.m. I was off again to fill sandbags for no. 2 right and left and to lay platforms in no. 2 right, so I had a party by Ludlow Castle, one in the hollow and one in no. 2 right. As the sun was awfully hot, and Pandy kept up a steady fire, unopposed, over the ground, it was very disagreeable. No. 1 left (which should have kept down the Kashmere for us) was blazing away in unextinguishable conflagration all the afternoon; our fire had ignited it. About five sleepy fellows sat down to mess.

11 September Up late, after dreaming that I was placing parties to work all night. At daybreak nos. 2 right and left opened and shut up the Kashmere and its neighbourhood. At 1 p.m. I was off again for 15 hours' duty, and with twelve sappers and 60 pioneers went to no. 2 right to make the traverses and epaulments longer. Enfilade [enemy fire from the flank] from right rear dreadful: the gun-wheels, carriages and trails were struck again and again; actually only one man (one of mine) killed. The battery banging away at the Kashmere. At 8 p.m. got another party: mending embrasures and lengthening epaulment.

12 September At daybreak got orders to open an embrasure in right epaulment − jolly time for such work; my six sappers and I on the

ALEX TAYLOR (1826-1912)
The storming of Delhi, underestimated at the time, was one of the great
military feats of the nineteenth century. Hugely outnumbered the British
assaulted walls 12' thick and 16' high; walls they had themselves
reinforced a few years before, and defended by superior guns with an
almost inexhaustible supply of ammunition. Who deserved credit for the
plan? Captain Alex Taylor, said Lang and his fellow Engineers. Over the
next sixty years Lang would frequently note in his diaries efforts made to
publicize Taylor's role. This drawing is of a statuette of him as he was then.
He died a general.

parapet got lots of grape plugged at us; all missed, but men in the batteries were hit. At 5.30 a.m. I was relieved by Medley. No. 3 did not open fire: *horresco referens!* they say that the embrasures don't bear! However, in a few hours all was rectified and they fired away. In the evening went to Observatory to watch the fire; all the batteries blazing away. Dined at mess (last time in that camp).

We are worked to the very limit of human power, and writing letters is almost impossible: to Lahore I send just a line to say daily I'm alive, and that is written at any moment, as I come into my tent after a night out, my eyes closing themselves and my senses quite foolish! I fling myself down with the sun up and am too tired to sleep, but restlessly again in excited dreams set parties to work under hot fire, howl at them, urge them on, grape pouring in, and loud guns drowning one's voice.

This is splendid, no nonsense about it. We are fighting close up now, hurrying on the most rapid of sieges, working recklessly under fire. Our big smashing guns roar out together in salvoes and crash into the crumbling walls. It does one good to hear and watch a salvo of 24-pounder guns pounding the walls, and making the 'deadly breach.'

13 September Up at 4.0 a.m. and relieved Medley in no. 2 right. A dreadfully hot day in that battery as Pandy had added heavy guns in that new battery in front of Kishanganj and his 24-pr balls walked through our traverses in reverse! It was fearful butchery, poor fellows mangled dreadfully. One rocket came in and mangled two Europeans in such style as I had never seen and have not seen since. They are most diabolical weapons.

The walls of Delhi were suffering severely. Both nos. 2 were knocking down the upper part of the wall 300 yards right and left of the Kashmere Bastion, breaching 50 feet of curtain on *our* left of Kashmere Bastion and somewhat of the face [of the Bastion].

In the evening Nicholson and Taylor came down and ordered me to inspect the breach after it got dark. I preferred going when I could see; so went at once to Kudsia Bagh, and, taking four riflemen, crossed the road leading to the river in front of Custom House and slunk up through some trees to foot of glacis.

Leaving my riflemen under a tree, I ran up the glacis and sat on the edge of the counterscarp and examined the appearance. The counterscarp is an earthen slope very steep about 18 feet deep; a ditch of 20 or 25 feet leads to a berm wall 8 feet high; opposite the curtain the berm is about 15 feet, but opposite the face it is narrow and the rubbish from the face falling left no berm. I ran back, fired at, and coming in was fired at by our own sentries.

Then I met Medley: he, I, Heathcote, with 26 of his Rifles, went off at 10 p.m. with a short ladder and a rod to measure. Medley, I, and four Rifles went to the edge of the ditch; they lay down and I slipped down to the bottom with the ladder: but go up I could not as Pandy was above chattering and whooping away; so after we had completely mastered all the details we went back: Medley rode to camp to report all practicable, as Greathed did, too, as to the Water Bastion's breach.

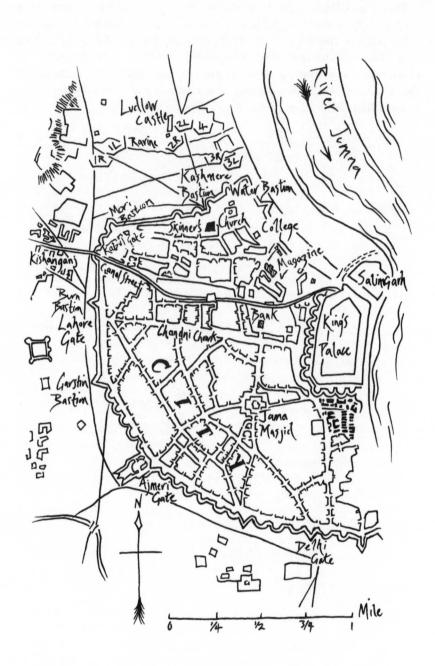

THE CITY OF DELHI, SEPTEMBER 1857

CHAPTER 7

The Assault

It is typical that nowhere in his letters or diaries does Lang make any reference either to the importance of his report on the breach or to the fact that others confidently expected that he would receive a VC for the work he did. Nor did he ever add further to the story, except, many years later, to explain that he only went in daylight because of his appallingly short sight! Others were less reticent.

Lang himself gives the incident a bare two paragraphs. The official biography of Alex Taylor gives it two pages with this conclusion. 'Alex Taylor and Frederick Maunsell recommended the hero of this feat for the Victoria Cross, and if Nicholson had lived Arthur Lang would surely have won this most coveted of personal honours, but the authorities considered that he had done nothing more than his duty. This was not the opinion of the camp, however, through which the news of the gallant exploit had run like wildfire; or of the Artillerymen, who had had almost enough and were watching for the moment when the breaches should be pronounced practicable and the order given to assault.'

'Had the camp been allowed to award one VC,' wrote Colonel Kendal Coghill, who was in 1857 the Adjutant of the 1st Bengal Fusiliers, 'the recipient of that honour would have been Arthur Lang, and that by universal acclamation. His gallantry on the 13th and 14th was heroic. He was attached to the storming party with which I served, and I saw him fighting like a paladin on the day following his more than gallant visit to the enemy's works, alone and in clear daylight.' Lang himself left only his own sketch of the breach and the following description of the storming party, of Nicholson's death, and of how near the British came to throwing away the fruits of their extraordinary assault.

89

14 September, Delhi At 2 a.m. I got orders to go to camp for instructions. There I found in our mess all our fellows preparing, reading their instructions, and poring over the big map of Delhi with various routes marked, buckling on revolvers, and storing haversacks with flasks and bread and snatching a few mouthfuls of supper by candlelight. Off I went and got a party of sappers with eighteen ladders and joined the 1st column (Nicholson's).

I had to lead 250 of the 1st Fusiliers up the face of the Kashmere Bastion, Medley to lead 75th up the breach. The 2nd column (Jones's) was to enter by the breach by Water Bastion, led by Greathed and Hovenden: reserve by Pemberton. 1 & 2 would then make the inner circuit of the walls.

No. 3 column (Campbell's) was to follow Home and Salkeld (who were to blow in the Kashmere Gate) up to Jama Masjid. No. 4 column (Reid's) led by Maunsell and Tennant were to take Kishanganj and Paharipur, enter Lahore Gate and up the Chandni Chowk.

Columns 1, 2 and 3 began to move (just before sunrise) from the road near Ludlow Castle. First rushed on No. 3, heads low and stooping forward, and running and cheering under showers of grape and musketry; then came Nicholson, with me and my party of 250 Fusiliers, with ladders.

At the Custom House Road we turned to the left and made up the glacis to the right face of the Bastion; it was most gloriously exciting; the bullets seemed to pass like a hissing sheet of lead over us, and the noise of the cheering was so great that I nearly lost my men, who doubled too far down the road before I could turn them, so they got more fire on the glacis than they needed: the edge of the ditch reached, down we slipped; just as I slid down, on my left I saw Medley and the 75th beginning to swarm their breach, and on my right I saw a column of smoke ascend and heard the explosion of the blowing in of the Kashmere Gate.

Up went our little ladder, but once on the berm we instantly saw that there was no place for placing our long ladders, so up we scrambled just a steep crumbling wall of masonry. I have seen it since in cold blood, and wondered how we got up at all. I was just falling backwards on our own bayonets when a Gurkha pushed me up luckily, and presently over we were, and, with the 75th and the men from the Water Bastion breach, were tearing down the ramp into the Main Guard behind the Kashmere Gate.

Here was a little confusion: no one exactly was sure of the way; Nicholson and Taylor ran up towards Skinner's House — wrong way — Pemberton and I and Captain Hay and a few more took the proper turning, under the ramparts along narrow lanes, ramparts on our right

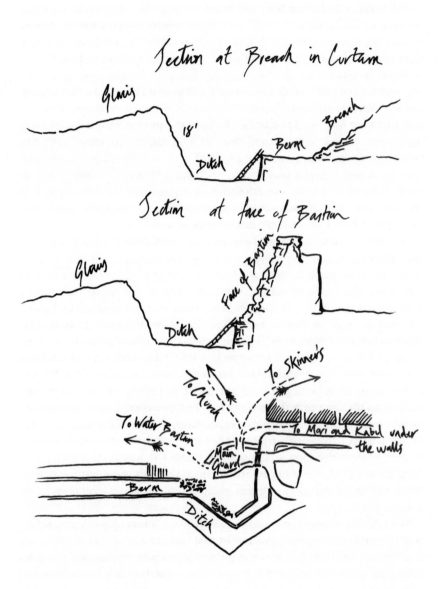

Section at Breach in Curtain

Glacis

18'

Ditch

Berm

Breach

Section at face of Bastion

Glacis

Face of Bastion

Ditch

To Skinner's

To Church

To Water Bastion

To Mori and Kabul under the walls

Main Guard

Berm

Ditch

**THE KASHMERE BREACH — as sketched by
A.M. Lang at the time of the assault**

91

and mud walls on our left, such a place, but on we rushed, shouting and cheering, while the grape and musketry from each bend, and from every street leading from our left, and from rampart and housetop, knocked down men and officers. It was exciting to madness and I felt no feeling except to rush on and hit: I only wondered how much longer I could possibly go on unhit, when the whole air seemed full of bullets.

We took tower after tower, and gun after gun, never stopping. On the Mori I shouted out to line the parapet and give three cheers; bad advice! for we were fired on from our own batteries: we tore strips of white, red and blue from dead Pandies' clothes, and put up an impromptu flag and then rushed along again. We seemed hardly to shoot any, but occasionally in some bend or in some tower caught fellows who were late in flying. I found that I was no hand at using a sword; I cut at several, but never gave a death blow; to my surprise I didn't seem able to cut hard, but it was of no consequence, as Gurkhas' kukri and Europeans' bayonet instantly did the business.

We poured past the Kabul Gate and we went swimmingly along until we nearly reached the Lahore; then a short check was given by a barricade with a gun firing grape from behind it. Brig Jones came up and called for the Engineer officer and asked where the Kabul Gate was. I answered. (Hovenden, Medley and Greathed were all wounded on glacis or breach, and as Taylor had gone astray with General Nicholson, Pemberton and I were only Engineers there. It was wonderful to me how I got so far all unhurt.) 'Far behind,' I said, 'We shall have the Lahore presently.' Alas, he declared that his orders were to stop at the Kabul.

We were all shouting for advance; but not a bit; all we could gain was to be allowed to hold our ground. But this was not so easy: as long as we rushed on, cheering and never stopping, all went well; but the check was sad: the men, crouching behind corners, and in the archways which support the ramparts, gradually nursed a panic. One by one they tried to get back: we stopped them and staved off the flight for half an hour, but at last out they all came and, sweeping back the officers, made for the Kabul Gate.

We held the Kabul Gate, and presently while I was up the Canal Street with a party, feeling our position in that direction, Nicholson collected a party and with Pemberton led up again towards the Lahore; the men who had once refused, refused again, and, turning, left Nicholson and Pemberton behind, who had to run before pursuing Pandies. I felt quite dispirited when I saw poor Nicholson, to whom we all trusted to get us on, brought back as we feared mortally wounded.

We didn't know how the other columns had fared, but meanwhile No. 4 had been totally defeated and repulsed from Kishanganj, leaving dead and wounded behind; Maunsell was dangerously wounded in the head.

As to No. 3, the corps had distinguished itself greatly. Home and two sappers had rushed to the Kashmere Gate and flung down powder against it, and then tumbled right and left away into the ditch; Salkeld rushed forward with the match; shot, he still went on, but with his arm nearly knocked off and his leg broken, he fell, throwing up the match gallantly and calling out to a sergeant to catch it; Sgt Carmichael seized it and ran up and was shot dead; Sgt Burgess then seized it and shared his fate; then Sgt Smith, more lucky, succeeded in lighting the slow match, and in went the Gate burying 30 Pandies behind it.

No. 3 (Tandy and Murray with it) made for the Jama Masjid but at the south of the Bank were repulsed: Tandy was killed, shot through the heart; and back fled No. 3 to the Church again.

That was the state of affairs on the evening of the 14th. That evening from the Kabul Gate, Col Burn took me and all the sappers I could find to pick our way from house to house. Pemberton had been taken off to camp, as he was wounded in the arm, as he and I were laying a mine to blow open the Kabul Gate, if required; so I was the only Engineer officer in that direction and I found out that I had been reported missing, the people at the Kashmere Gate not knowing who were at the Kabul.

Col Burn and I went on taking several houses, first getting on the roof, firing on any inside the next yard; then the sappers would pick a doorway through a wall and in we would go, turn out the old men, women and children, and make that house safe, and so on to the next, going, obliquely, eastward. Having established an advanced picket in a serai and adjoining house, as it was very late we stopped and down I fell at once where I was and slept. I was completely done up, and I could not speak, having lost my voice entirely from shouting and cheering during the morning.

15 September Next morning we continued the picking through house principle, but, getting on too far, we had to fall back. Pemberton, having had his wound dressed, came back, as the corps was so inefficient that the slightly wounded had to come on duty at once. We erected parapets on the rooftops with gaily painted doors and sandbags, and made a parapet for a 12-pr gun on the rampart which we turned inwards on the Lahore Gate.

Some of the houses in Canal Street are very pretty: courts in the centre of them with little canals and fountains, shrubs, flowers and creepers; balconied rooms, gorgeous in barbaric style of gilding and glass; immense mirrors, thick rich carpets and comfortable chairs, elegant furniture, and a scent of attar all about. Strange it seemed to see these rooms full of rough soldiers, Europeans and Sikhs. I lay down in the street that night with a low wall of sandbags at my head to save me from bullets.

16 September Next morning the 61st took the Magazine, and I went to the Kashmere Gate to Colonel Baird Smith. He was lying in pain with a sprained arm, and Taylor was done up by fatigue and fever, so Home was acting Chief Engineer. Home is worshipped by generals. It is grand what a position we Engineer subs have: we give our opinions more coolly and forcibly than any colonels would dare to do to generals and they all tacitly agree that we are the managing minds. Were it not for us nearly nothing would be done. We seem to propose, arrange and carry out everything.

Home set me to superintend the works in the College and Magazine, where we were putting up a battery to peg away at Salimgarh; heavy and light mortars, too, were playing into the Palace and Salimgarh. In the evening I rode out of the Kashmere Gate into our new camp at the south end of Metcalfe Park, and felt intensely delighted to see the few survivors.

List of wounded and killed on the 14th: Tandy − killed; Salkeld − wounded dangerously (since died); Greathed, Chesney, Maunsell, Brownlow, Hovenden, − wounded severely; Medley, Home, Pemberton − wounded slightly; Gustavinski − wounded in shoulder.

Since I came on duty at 4.0 a.m. on the 13th, alone of all my corps I had never come off duty, and most intensely thankful I ought to be to God for having spared me thru' all the dangers of the storming and street fighting, for the strength to stand all the long fatigue and the work. The happiness I felt again at returning to my few remaining comrades, to clean clothes and clean sheets, to rest and quiet, I can't express.

17 September On the morning of the 17th, the 52nd took the Bank − walked quietly into it − but no further advance was made. I fancy that the drunkenness of the Europeans prevents an advance. Though hundreds of rupees' worth of beer, wines and spirits are smashed, still the men get drunk. On the night of the 16th/17th, ten men were caught while lying drunk in a house, bound, tortured, and cut to pieces. Yet this does not deter our men.

18 September Last night I rode to the old camp and saw Chesney and my comrade of the breach, Medley, both poor wounded men. I then went to see Dacres and stayed to dine with him at the Plunger mess. He is writing by my side here in our mess tent, as are Murray, Ward and Forbes: we are under a lemiana, a cool breeze blowing thru', and the pretty park about us: it is like a picnic, only the sound of heavy mortars shelling Salimgarh and the Palace is rather more warlike than peaceful.

Today was the eclipse of the sun which all saw plainly, a dim moonlight at 9 a.m. Another advance was made on the Lahore Gate and again were our gallant (?) fellows repulsed. Poor Briscoe of the 75th was killed. When I left the Kabul Gate, only Captain Drew and Lieutenants Justice and Briscoe remained 'unexpended' in the 75th, and now one of them is gone.

Out of our 27 Engineer officers, Taylor, Ward, Thackeray and I were alone unhurt who went in on the 14th, but Geneste and Forbes have since come off sick list, and the slightly wounded (Home, Champain, Murray and Pemberton) have to come on the roster. Taylor won't let any more of us lead parties as the Engineer Brigade is barely efficient now and not another can be hit.

The city reports as to where the Pandies are gone are, of course, various and lying. Some say that the great mass have marched to join the Gwalior troops, leaving a few to hold us in check a few days, that they may have a good start. Some men I seized on the night of the 14th/15th declared that two or three regiments had marched in full strength across the bridge. I really think that both Meerut and Agra are threatened, while a few Ghazis [Mohammedan fanatics] keep us at bay on these streets.

I went this evening and paid Brigadier Jones a visit in his little house near Kabul Gate and he showed me a plan of the houses through which he would advance tomorrow morning. They are advancing house by house along that zigzag street from Canal Street to the Chandni Chowk. At present both columns 1 and 2 are under Brigadier Jones, at and beyond the Kabul Gate.

19 September This morning I was again sent to help at the Kabul Gate, and there again joined Brig Jones. I found that we held most of the Canal Street, and at Jung Bahadur's house which is on the right of the street, about a quarter of a mile up, we had a very strong picket. Meeting Taylor and Fred Roberts [a Gunner Lt, later Lord Roberts of Kandahar] there, I went with them down a street to the right and we began to make our way, breaking into houses, across or down lanes, occupying and loopholing commanding houses, till we commanded the interior of the Burn Bastion (just north of Lahore Gate) and subsequently cut off a mortar which they had in the lane below the ramparts.

I broke open a door connecting with that lane, and 50 Europeans and 50 Sikhs being formed up, they were ordered to cross about 10 feet of lane to the ramp which led into the Bastion. Just as the first men began to start, *one* Pandy musket was fired, on which back rushed our gallant fellows and all fired their pieces in the air! Such curs has this sort of fighting made them. We again soothed and encouraged the fools and then in we went without losing a man, and at last held the Bastion at which we had fatally failed on the 14th when carrying all before us.

I immediately began to pull down Pandy's sandbag parapets with the Europeans and Sikhs and made a parapet and barricade across the lane, and getting afterwards some sappers, made a parapet at the head of the ramp, behind which we put a light gun. Although they fired grape and musketry into the Bastion during the night, only two men were wounded.

Just after we had rushed into the Bastion a Pandy strolled up the ramp. At the top an officer clapped a hand on his shoulder saying 'Kaun hai?' [Who is it?] The startled scoundrel, with a ludicrous expression of dismay, asked 'Yih Angrezi guard hai?' [Is this an English guard?] Our friend was disarmed and shot; he had confessed he was a Ghazi and had been out spying and came back to tell his friends that Europeans and Sikhs were coming; rather late his information!

20 September Before daybreak I was off again with 25 of the 2nd Europeans (that I think the best fighting regiment here) and 25 of the Queen's Sikhs. The minarets of the Fateporah Masjid were my beacons and towards them I made my way, occupying commanding houses and opening ways into houses and through lanes. After some hours' crafty sapping I peered over the parapet wall of a roof and saw opposite me the Fateporah Masjid across the street, and below me the deserted Chandni Chowk; to my right I saw the Lahore Gate and two or three officers and men emerging, having sapped their way there.

We might have entered the Gate the night before; for Fred Roberts and I had taken a Brahmin (leaving about 20 more, to be shot if our man played false) and made him take us to his house just by the Lahore Gate. From a window we looked down on the two guns (a 24-pounder at the Gate, and a 6-pounder pointing up the street), two sentries by them, three or four lounging about cleaning their arms; otherwise the street was deserted; however, Taylor declared that we should take it without losing one man, and the event has most fully justified him.

All was deserted before us. I ran back, got Willes and his 25 of the 2nd Europeans, and what Sikhs I could rescue from looting the last big house I had occupied, and we descended into the street and marched our gallant little army up the grand but deserted Chandni Chowk, finding none but dead and wounded Pandies, and wondering at our finding our way all clear before us. We marched straight up to the Lahore Gate of the Palace; there I spied through chinks in the great big doors and saw four great guns, crammed to the muzzle with grape, pointing, within ten feet of the door. I went back for powder; meanwhile Home had been coming with some and while I was away he blew in the Gate.

In the Palace Murray and a Rifle private raced to sit first in the crystal throne of the Moghuls in the Diwan-i-Khas [Hall of Private Audience]. British soldiers and Sikhs rummaged all the swell private rooms and marble baths of the Zenana [women's quarters]. All the valuables seemed to have been taken away, and what was left the troops seized and tossed about. I took a little book which I *say* was a present from the Prince of Bokhara to the Delhi family! It was in an elegant private room in the Zenana; there I took too five pachisi [an Indian game similar to ludo] markers of glass which young princesses had been playing with just before their flight: but no real valuable plunder are we allowed to take.

I joined a party bound for Jama Masjid and we took that unopposed. We went up the minaret and saw the whole city and country like a map below our feet; all Delhi was ours.

Our Cavalry rode round the walls, and a small force, just for the name of the thing, marched to and occupied the Delhi Gate. Taylor rode his horse up the steps of Jama Masjid, we danced about, drank beer and brandy, and Sikhs lit fires in the sacred mosque: Geneste and I sent sappers for ladders and took down the two sacred Roe's eggs: I have one now.

We (Engineer officers) then rode to congratulate Col Baird Smith and to drink champagne to our conquest, conquerors in the most memorable siege and storm of Delhi.

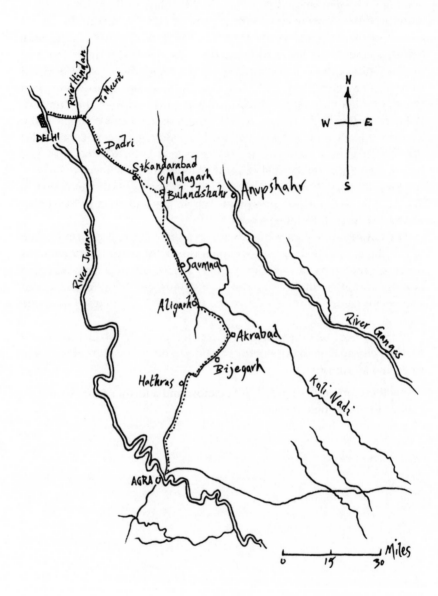

THE ROUTE OF THE COLUMN, SEPTEMBER/OCTOBER 1857

CHAPTER 8

In Pursuit

As one of few unwounded members of the Engineer Brigade, Lang was immediately posted to a new Movable Column commanded by Colonel Greathed which was sent out in pursuit of those sepoys who had fled the city. He was consequently to find himself involved with the next great campaign of the Mutiny year: the second relief of Lucknow.

Although no one at Delhi knew it at the time, the first relief of Lucknow was completed only a day or two after the fall of Delhi. This first relieving force was led by General Havelock, who had first recaptured Cawnpore, and then after a series of brilliant battles forced a way through to the Residency. Sadly he arrived too late to save Sir Henry Lawrence who had died in July. Sadly too he had insufficient troops to bring out those besieged there. His column was therefore also stranded in Lucknow and a further force would have to go to their rescue.

This second relief force would be led by a Crimean veteran sent out from England, Sir Colin Campbell. Sir Colin's forces, however, would not reach Cawnpore until November, when they would link up with those troops that could be spared from Delhi. Meanwhile Greathed, and his successor Hope Grant, unaware at first of Havelock's predicament, would pursue those who fled from Delhi, and try to bring to battle the perpetrator of the Cawnpore massacre, Nana Sahib, and the eight thousand troops who had mutinied at the cantonment of Gwalior.

22 September, Jhajjar Nawab's Palace, Delhi As I am off again tomorrow morning, with the pursuing column after the scoundrels of Pandies, I must write you a few lines from Delhi, where I now sit, one of the conquerors! This same Palace is a very ordinary two-storied house, just south of the King's Palace and near the river bank. I must say that it is a very cool and airy abode, refreshing after our camp on that malarious plain across the Ridge.

Early this morning the Engineer Brigade moved in to this place and I got orders that a pursuing column under Col Greathed (Home and I as Engineers, with Lt Stevenson of the Sappers and a small park) was to march in pursuit this evening. I am afraid that for the next (how long?) I must give up hoping for either receiving or sending letters. I fancy Anupshahr is our destination, but of course it depends on what we find en route. Perhaps we shall meet and join Havelock's army when it has relieved Lucknow, or even be a part of some grand army which Sir Colin Campbell may command in person.

I must say that I would now — having ceased to be a carpet knight, having worked hard at a siege, led a storming party and fought through the streets of Delhi — like to return to my little lady-love at Lahore and rest on my laurels and enjoy love instead of war. However, it is ordered differently and a longer separation from my wife-to-be is a trial I must not a moment deplore when I have been so mercifully preserved through excessive dangers and fatigue from sword and pestilence.

Today I rode up the Chandni Chowk and saw three bodies laid out. These were two sons and a grandson of the King.

On the 21st Hodson had ridden out with a handful of Plungers to a place about 6 miles south of this and captured the King and Queen. On the 22nd he rode out and found these three princes with about 300 followers. (Orders have been given that no princes are to be brought in alive.) The followers surrendered, but Hodson trapped the princes in their carriage a short way from their men, interposed his Plungers, set off the carriage at full gallop, till he had got out of sight of the Shazada's [Indian Prince's] men. Then he made the three get out and strip off their glorious array, then shot them, and brought the bodies in.

At the Ajmeri Gate I found young Charlie Boileau with his regiment (61st) again, having left the Artillery when he heard that his regiment was to join the column. I found him fuming with wrath and vexation, as his regiment had been declared too weak to go, and had been cut out by the 75th. I am very sorry for this. I was in hope too that Dacres might come; but Hugh Gough and Baker are the two officers with the Plungers whom we carry off with us.

September 24, Near the River Hindan Home and I dined at the Engineer mess and said goodbye to our comrades on the 22nd; however, it was not until 3 a.m. yesterday that I could get my servants and camels (which they crushed down with their bundles of loot) to start. We went to our camp outside Ajmeri Gate, which I expected to find struck; but there it lay dark, and I, failing to find my proper locale, flung myself down to sleep till daybreak. I then heard that we were to halt, which news pleased worn-out me very much.

Our column paraded in the evening:

2 Troops Horse Artillery [Remmington's and Blunt's]

1 Light Field Battery, Artillery

50 Sappers and 2 Companies, 10th and 11th, Punjab Sappers.

9th Lancers

Squadrons of 1st, 2nd and 4th Punjab Cavalry

Hodson's Plungers

The Multani Horse

H.M.'s 8th and 75th regiments

2nd (Green's), and 4th (Wilde's) Punjab Infantry

At 3 a.m. we marched back in at Lahore Gate, up Chandni Chowk, out at Calcutta Gate, over the bridge of boats, then two clear miles to the suspension bridge over the Hindan river, and then another mile to camping ground. No trees sheltered us, and as our tents were not up till the afternoon (mine, one of the first, was not up till 3 p.m.) the sun touched us up as we lay out unsheltered. Luckily our mess came up at 11. Some regiments got no food, and the bread for the troops only came up at 8 p.m. The Artillery did not get dinner till 9. The Lancers got none! We shall do better in future.

This is different work to the jolly 'peace' marches when half way you find the chota hazri by the roadside, coffee, tea and curacoa, and on arrival at your camping ground there is the mess tent with breakfast all ready when you shall have bathed and dressed.

The principal care of the day in such a life as this is to get one's breakfast early; (without plates, knives or forks, we eat away in picnicking fashion;) and the next to get the shelter of one's tent as soon as possible: these two points gained, the soldier is satisfied, and living only for the day does not care what comes next, but eats and sleeps as much and whenever he can.

I have pitched my tent without kanauts [tent-walls], and a cool breeze blows through, pleasant enough. I am very glad that we have left that pestilential Delhi with its odours of scents, spices and dead bodies. Here at least we shall, while marching, have fresh air and change, and a week hence it will be October, which I look on the first of the cold weather months — it is certainly so in the Punjab.

This time last year we had begun cricket at Lahore. When shall we have those jolly days again? It seems to me as if war, discomfort, and this unsettled state will last another year, and it will be very long before such a state of things as existed in the civilized happy India of 56/57 will be seen again.

We march at 3 a.m. tomorrow for Dadri towards Bulandshahr and the Fort of Malagarh which we are to take and destroy. We carry entrenching tools for 500 men and ladders for escalading.

26 September, Dadri We got in here between 8 and 9, and set fire to Dadri as soon as we arrived, as it is a rebellious village. It is blazing and smoking away. This cool breeze, which refreshes us, spreads the conflagration.

We hear that Walidad Khan is attacking some villages 30 miles from here, the scoundrel; I hope he will defend Malagarh, that we may kill him and every soul that follows his green standard.

We are all getting pretty confident that we are bound for Lucknow and an Oudh campaign with the main army, as we have so much Cavalry and Horse Artillery, of which Havelock and Sir Colin are so much in want.

27 September, Sikandarabad We marched at 2 a.m. and marched 12 miles into Sikandarabad, and hearing that the Nana Sahib and Walidad Khan were at Bulandshahr with a lot of their ruffians and the 12th N.I. and the 14th Irregulars (the most atrocious and barbarous of the rebel regiments) we had orders to march on again at 2 p.m. This order was cancelled and 7 p.m. was settled as the starting hour. By which arrangement we should have come on the enemy in the dark or else have had to lay out all night on the damp grass and under the dew at Bulandshahr for nothing! Luckily this order too was cancelled, and 2 a.m. was the order.

28 September, Bulandshahr According to my usual custom I started on my horse for the march and, as soon as the column was fairly off, I dismounted and walked near the head of the column till nearly dawn, and then, sitting down, let most of it march by, and so changing my society walked with some of the rearguard.

I was so walking with Wilde's Corps when rumours came down from the front that we were coming on the enemy, so I jumped instanter on my horse and galloped to the front, just in time to join Murray (Horse Artillery) who with two guns, escorted by a troop of Lancers and squadron of 1st Punjab Cavalry, was going to advance. It appeared that as Fred Roberts [now Assistant Quartermaster General], with an escort of Punjab Cavalry, was feeling his way ahead, to mark out a camp at Bulandshahr, just before dawn a sentry challenged his men:-

Rebel: Who goes there?

Answer: Sowars.

Rebel: What regiment?

Answer: What's *your* regiment?

Rebel: Fourteenth.

On which a bullet sent the sentry flying.

Well, on we went along the fine smooth pukka road, over which arched the boughs of the sissoo and sirris. This shady road led to the civil station of Bulandshahr, and then forking led to the city. At the point of the V a hasty parapet had been thrown up, behind which two or three guns were placed, and other guns stood about. However, this we found out afterwards, for the compounds and roads so abound in trees that we could see nothing. 'Now,' said the guide, '500 yards ahead are the enemy.' Round swung Murray's two guns and the jolly order, 'Load with ball,' was given! Joyful sound! Again the blood danced in one's veins like mercury and I could have laughed with pleasure.

The Lancers filed into the open ploughed land on our right and Remmington called out, 'Let's have first shot'. But no sooner was the word out of his mouth when 'bang' went Pandy's gun, and 'whishhh' came the 9-pounder ball ricocheting like a cricket ball along the smooth hard road: delightful; for just a week we had ceased to hear the perpetual sound of ball. Our two guns answered immediately, and the smoke curled up blue and purple against the rising sun. Hammer and tongs they went, the arching boughs crashing and falling across the road and the enemy's balls bounding along the road.

Up galloped the three other guns of Remmington's Troop, and, wheeling to the right into the ploughed land, formed line and let fly at the smoke of the enemy's guns. The 1st Punjab Cavalry galloped away to the right and the Lancers to the left, and Bourchier's five 9-pounders and one 24-pounder howitzer, with eight horses to each, flew across the ploughed fields as if they were Light Horse Artillery and took Pandy in flank. Two guns of Blunt's Troop took position on an open cutcha road through the fields on our left: so in twenty minutes we had 13 guns pegging away at Pandy's five or six; but then he knew the ground and could fire straight at us, whereas we were throwing shot and shell at an invisible foe (and wasting ammunition?).

Presently we knew that the 1st Punjab Cavalry were engaged by the return of Captain Best with a deep wound across his neck – he ran a sowar through, who writhed up the blade and slashed Best's neck nearly through! Meanwhile the 8th, 75th and Green's Corps had been marching up to our right, keeping hidden as much as possible. Fifty of Green's men who had been with the guns had seized one of the station houses on the

FRED ROBERTS (1832-1914)
A friend of Lang throughout their lives, Fred Roberts founded a great
military career on his work in the Mutiny; the kind of career that friends
had expected Lang to pursue. Lang rose to Colonel; Roberts to
Field-Marshal. Lang was an engineer first and a soldier for convenience.
Roberts was a soldier first and last. At Addiscombe he had the less
distinguished career, but he devoted his first years in India to perfecting
his talents as a staff officer, and through determination, and gallantry, he
made himself indispensable. He remained so until his death, still a serving
officer, in the First World War.

right, and after some time our Infantry, with a great deal of cheering and no results, and a great deal of Delhi musketry, took a couple of guns (which Pandy had abandoned!), one a good English 9-pounder and one a native long 3-pounder.

Up the two 'V' roads galloped Guns and Cavalry. On the left at the open gateway of the long half-serai, half-street, Tonnochy Ganj, Cracklow worked a gun in most plucky style, tho' soon, with two horses killed, one Artillery man killed and five wounded, only two men were working the gun. Green's men were supporting him, doing lots of wild musketry. On the right the Lancers charged through the street from the right to the left, doing little execution but fired upon from side streets and having lots of men and horses knocked over and four officers wounded.

The 8th had charged to the right and Gough and Younghusband (Hodson's Plungers and Punjab Cavalry) had killed each their 40 or 50 of the enemy, and nearly taken two guns, which the 8th had pointed out to Hugh Gough, who having his eyeglass broken by a ball, could not see and galloped the wrong way! Then the 9th Lancers, a couple of guns and the 8th charged through Tonnochy Ganj, and except catching and shooting Pandies in the streets the action was over.

With a few sowars I galloped over the bridge to reconnoitre the ground. Pandy had got clear away, though his course was marked by a few deserted gharis [carts], a palka-ghari [covered cart] and red coats of the N.I. thrown off in flight.

Fred Roberts joined me, we found a place for camp and our troops crossed over. I for one was not sorry for breakfast, considering we marched at 2 and had been fighting from sunrise till noon. It was a very pretty sight, and as an independent staff officer I could be about everywhere, right, centre and left, propose an order to Colonel Greathed and immediately gallop off to carry it. Our loss was 47 killed and wounded: no officer killed, but three dangerously and two slightly wounded.

That evening at Colonel Greathed's tent we were assembling a reconnoitring party to ride to Malagarh, five miles off, when in came news that the Fort was abandoned — rather a relief to Home and me!

1 October, Malagarh Here I am seated in the cool open room over the river gateway of the stronghold of that scoundrel Walidad Khan (nephew of the King of Delhi and levyer of blackmail and stopper of daks between Aligarh and Meerut). Here are also Home and Stevenson and Hugh Gough: our garrison consists of a detachment of Hodson's Horse, the 10th and 11th companies of the Punjab Sappers and 50 true sappers.

This is our third day here and our occupation is the demolition of this Fort: we live very well on plunder, on the geese, ducks, and pigeons of Walidad, from whose stores we are also well provided with tables and chairs and plates and dishes; beautiful beer, unlimited in quantity; cones on cones of lump sugar, and numberless great yellow bottles of rose water with which we bathe! In fact we are living in style, conquerors and marauders. Our camp, from which we are detached, is five miles off on this (the left) bank of the Kali Nadi opposite Bulandshahr, where they rest after the toils of battle and make very tardy arrangements for sending the sick and wounded back to Delhi or Meerut.

Colonel Greathed, with his staff and an escort of Cavalry, rode here on 29 September. It was most pleasant riding in the cool early morning, under shady trees and over smooth turf. The country about is very well wooded and green and pretty. How delighted I felt when I saw the Fort and knew it was deserted and that we had not to take it. Our light guns would have been of no avail against the high thick earthen ramparts. It has a very strong profile indeed, this Malagarh. It is rectangular, with round bastions (still higher than the ramparts) and has three gateways all round — no end of corners. I should say it had, for we have levelled a long line of rampart, burned one gateway, and blown in another.

Home and I, with the rest of the staff, went over the place, saw Walidad's own apartments; those of his ladies, his mosque, and his strange native guns (his good ones he has taken away). Some of the grape was telegraph wire, cut into pieces and put into leather bags. Some guns were made from the screw-pile ends of telegraph posts.

I took as loot a large, but impure, cornelian, the size of a plum, and a pretty little painted box. My servants got me five dozen of first-rate beer, two great cones of loaf sugar, a very good cane bed etc.

Home stayed here and I rode back and got Stevenson and all the sappers and pickaxes, shovels etc. We had a capital device to collect coolies. We let the villagers come in, some two or three hundred, to loot; laden with plunder they came to pass out of the gates, but our sentries stopped them, lightened them of their loads and provided each man with a pickaxe, shovel or spade, and sent them on to the ramparts to work!

We don't seem likely to knock ourselves up by hard marching: Greathed seems to like an independent command, and will potter about in districts where no senior officer can supersede him. We shall wait at Bulandshahr till our sick and wounded get back and more ammunition comes out.

We are just going to blow in a bit of glacis and the bastion by the gateway. They are great fun these explosions and we try to get Gough, or any visitors, into places where they will get doses of earth and dust, without being really hurt.

2 October, Malagarh Yesterday the gateway, bastion and the escarp [side of the ditch below the walls] were very successfully blown in. The last mine to be blown in was the counterscarp, by which we should make a broad smooth road into the place. Stevenson and I rushed up on the ruins of the bastion and saw Home run laughing up to the mine: he put his hand out and to our horror instantaneously the mine sprung; down we rushed, put every man to work to scrape and dig. Sergeant Robson, a few feet from poor Home, had been knocked down and bruised, but was not really injured, but of poor Home for a minute or two we saw no traces. I looked round a little distance and about twenty yards off in the hollow of a well I recognised his body, all mangled and covered with dust: poor fellow, his legs were broken in two places, his arms broken and one nearly torn off; his death must have been instantaneous.

It was like a horrid dream from which I longed to wake. I could not realise that merry Home, so full of life and happiness just before, was now dead. He so enjoyed these explosions, laughing always as he watched us clear off. He had escaped the dangers of the blowing in of the Kashmere Gate, to meet his end before a deserted fort.

I wrote to his brother, and to Taylor, and to camp. I reported the fortress as rendered quite indefensible, as the parapet all round was removed, and a broad smooth road made across the ditch.

Colonel Greathed came out to look at the Fort today and agreed that enough was done. After breakfast we turned everybody and everything to be preserved out of the place and set fire to all the buildings and blew up the powder houses, which made a most grand explosion.

4 October, Saumna Yesterday, we marched at 2 a.m. Moon full, or nearly so; shone the whole march till daybreak, soon after which we encamped. We breakfasted among the trees of a garden and voted it like a picnic: these cool mornings, which are now coming on, are very pleasant. At work at adjustment of poor Home's affairs. A cossid [messenger] from Lucknow came in, who said all was well at Lucknow on 24 August; that Havelock was marching northwards; that two regiments of sepoys held Aligarh. Marched at 2 a.m.; got into camp at Saumna soon after sunrise.

5 October, Aligarh Again on Monday a fight! After a beautiful moonlight march we came up to Aligarh city about 7; our advanced cavalry drew fire from the gates of the town.

The sun was well up, and the glare, smoke, and masses of trees, prevented the view being good. I recognised at once the strange report of the telegraph screw-pile guns and telegraph wire grape.

As at Bulandshahr some artillery and cavalry advanced on the right by a road leading to the city and on the left across the fields to get round the city. Right, centre, and left I visited in succession, to see who was at each place and what was before them. While on the left, I heard that on the right an advance had been made and a gun or two taken. Off I galloped and about 300 yards from one of the city gates found some of our guns, a troop of Lancers, 8th and Green's.

However, it was a case of halt; so presently Lane and I with 50 Sikhs went forward to reconnoitre and look at a gun which appeared deserted at the city gate; at 150 yards a man rushed out and fired a dose of grape at us which knocked over one Sikh and then they closed the gates. The Artillery called out for a clear road and we went right and left, and they fired to no purpose ahead.

I went on the roof of what seemed a chapel, a little ahead, to spy, but there were so many trees that I could make out nothing. Meanwhile our respected commander had come up and sagely remarking that it was not safe to run one's head against stone walls, actually insisted that this column should turn and follow the other left column, in fact that we should turn our backs on one gun. Even the European Infantry were amazed and I heard them saying that on seeing the smoke of the gun once they would be on it before it could fire again. I was so ashamed that I could take no more pleasure or interest in the affair. We were halted, and sat in inglorious inactivity, sulkily eating our breakfasts, while we envied the left column which, of course, unrestrained, was doing good work.

Probyn and his 2nd Punjab Cavalry first returned from their gallop on our right, having killed some 50 of the enemy; then returned Major Ouvry [commanding the cavalry] and Roberts, who had all the fun: they had pursued for about five miles southwards, and Watson's 1st Punjab Cavalry had killed nearly 300, chiefly infantry: few sepoys, but Mussalman scoundrels, armed and flying for Akrabad. The Lancers had started with these Punjab Irregulars, but in four miles had lost one-and-a-half miles! So much for their qualifications as *Light* Cavalry.

By now the 75th were on the other side of the town and entering it at their pleasure. By way of a neat finish to the affair, Green's men were sent through and about the town, and we encamped on this northern front of the place, I suppose to entice anyone to reoccupy Aligarh, and nullify this morning's work. However, as our casualties were nothing, and about 400 of Mussalman fanatics and sepoys have been killed and we have a few telegraph guns, a largish wrought-iron and a small brass native gun, it will appear as if we had done well.

Tomorrow we march on Akrabad, but I fancy Watson's sowars must have established so wholesome a dread that the fugitives won't consider Akrabad far enough. The health of the troops is capital: the march has wonderfully diminished the list of sick with which we started.

Heard from Sarah that Elliot Brownlow had passed through and paid them a long visit on the 1st, and was going on at once; I hope I may see the old boy immediately; and nothing is more probable, I think. Sarah writes great praise of him and her pleasure at meeting him.

6 October, Akrabad Marched at 3. Fourteen miles into Akrabad. Crossed the canal just where it branches into two – a most splendid canal it looked, with its broad volume of water, green grass slopes and shady trees all along the banks.

The Irregular Cavalry preceded the column and killed about 50 fugitives from Akrabad, among them the scoundrel Mangal Singh and his brother Mehtab Singh, both very fine large men, and to see their bodies in a garden beyond the town a great many of our fellows went out during the day. Our men showed more cruelty in their treatment of the few poor remaining wretches in the town than I have ever seen.

I received orders at noon to burn and destroy the place, and so went in with a company of sappers for about four or five hours.

8 October, Bijegarh Here we are encamped on a fine open plain. The fort at Bijegarh was set fire to by some fellows, to the anger of Greathed. The town seems Hindu and the people very civil.

9 October, Hathras At 2.0 a.m. resumed our march over cutcha roads, about 12 miles, then came on the pukka road to Hathras. A message came in from Fraser, Civilian and Military Governor of the North-West Provinces, (the Engineers come to the fore in a crisis) ordering us in to Agra at once.

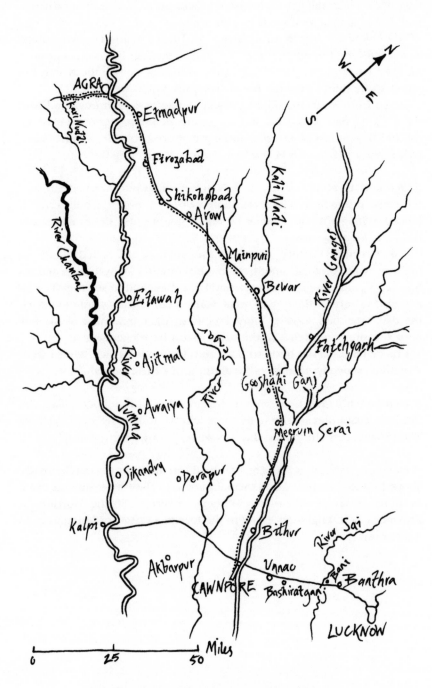

THE ROUTE OF THE COLUMN, OCTOBER 1857

110

CHAPTER 9

From Agra to Cawnpore

Greathed's rather dilatory pursuit of the mutineers now took his column towards Lucknow by way of two of the great cities of the North-West Provinces. To the heroes of Delhi the two cities could hardly have presented a sharper contrast.

Agra, which Lang had visited in wonder only a few years before on his way to Lahore, had survived the worst of the Mutiny almost entirely by good luck. Good management had been notoriously lacking, but the British had managed to take refuge successfully within the Fort. Agra's administration and its society still retained much of the liberal style of the North-West Provinces which clearly both charmed and irritated those who came fresh from the horrors of Delhi. Agra's luck held. Greathed's column was to arrive just in time to save Agra from the attack they most feared — that of the Gwalior Contingent.

Cawnpore's story was very different. Though the garrison had been commanded by a distinguished general in Sir Hugh Wheeler, he had been tricked by the Nana Sahib into a withdrawal that had resulted in a massacre of men, women and children. When Cawnpore was recaptured, Havelock's second-in-command, Brigadier-General Neill, insisted that in future every soldier should be taken on a tour of the sites of Wheeler's last stand, and of the massacre of the women and children. It was no surprise that those troops who now passed through Cawnpore left it with a cold, bitter determination to exterminate the mutineers. Lang was just one of thousands who saw what he saw, and felt what he felt.

10 October, Agra We marched all night from Hathras, and soon after sunrise we saw the river before us, the bridge of boats, and beyond that the towering red walls of the Fort and the city of Agra, and to the left the beautiful Taj.

Didn't we come in proudly, the elite of the Delhi army! The ramparts were lined with the imprisoned Agra population, the 3rd Europeans in red and pipeclay (unwonted sight!) and fair sex (actually bonnets and parasols) cheering as each regiment crossed over the bridge and under the walls. The Agra people really seemed a different race to us Punjabis. True North-Westers, they wore black coats and black hats and stared at Europeans in *khaki,* wondered at those foreigners the Sikhs and at the martial cut-throats of Green's and Wilde's. These two last came in with bands playing and marching beautifully, steady and strong, after their 31-mile march (Europeans had had gharis and elephants).

The men went on to camp on the parade ground. I (with many other officers) went into the Fort, to coffee-shop, swimming bath, and breakfast in the society of Ladies! The Ladies have a mess at 'Buckingham Palace', where live Lady Outram, Mrs Glover, Mrs Machell etc. (You knew Mrs Machell as Miss Nuthall; we instantly struck up an acquaintanceship, having played together in infancy at Cheltenham!). Fancy seeing Ladies again: we were so jolly, and sitting after breakfast with them, it seemed that days of peace had returned. Then, as Mrs Glover was showing me the latest *Illustrated London News,* suddenly a frantic Agra man, unused to gunfire, rushed in to say that they were fighting hammer and tongs in camp.

On went swords, and we were off. I saw the 3rd Europeans falling in, the gates closed, and through the wicket pouring inwards pale-faced Keranies and their ladies who had ventured out to see their relievers. With difficulty, I got a gate open and galloped away as fast as I could thro' non-combatants, camels and baggage. Luckily I didn't meet the Agra Volunteer Horse, who on seeing the enemy's cavalry fled so precipitately that they smashed men and horses of our side and spread wild alarm!

At last I reached the parade ground and emerging saw some of our camp pitched, and the khets [fields] beyond full of smoke and reports, so that I could not make the fight out. I saw Norman [Adjutant-General to the column] gallop up, sword in hand, and shout out to me, 'Look out, cut that scoundrel down.' Funny place, thought I, the rear of camp, to cut anyone down — when I descried a grey-jacketed, light-cavalryman scouring along between me and the tents, closely pursued by a red-coated sowar (of Probyn's 2nd Punjabis, I thought). Watching the pair, I saw, too late, that they were allies and I dashed in pursuit; they passed two regiments of infantry who fired volleys without touching them and they got clear away.

It appears that a great number of the 1st Light Cavalry and of a red-coated Irregular regiment (they say 2nd Gwalior Cavalry) charged from left to right of our camp in rear, killing numbers of camp followers and some fighting men: they, for a moment, took one of Blunt's guns, but were driven off by the Lancers. Four of the enemy also came in as jugglers to the quarter-guard tent of the Lancers, suddenly killed a sergeant and wounded a trooper, and then were themselves polished off.

How did it happen? It seems that the Mhow Brigade had crossed the Chambal and Kari Nuddi, and were encamped between four and five miles from Agra on the Gwalior road. A lot of scoundrels had agreed to effect the smashing of the bridge, so as to prevent succour, and then Agra was to be attacked. They had some enormous guns – great native brass 18 and 24-pounders – so you may imagine the time it took them to cross the rivers.

They had a spy on the bridge till 12 at night who reported that no troops were coming; so when our tents commenced to be pitched, the enemy thought the Agra garrison had come out and were going to the camp. In consequence, up they moved through the high crops, opened fire into camp, the balls crashing through tents and knocking over men and horses; and their cavalry charged through camp.

Oh, the good intelligence we get: tahsildars [revenue officers] coming to report the enemy 20 miles off, in full flight, just when the guns opened fire on our camp! I bet that tahsildar is (according to the civilians) still a faithful and valued servant: 'Poor fellow, how could he know better, being a native!'

The Artillery and Cavalry, with their Delhi experience, turned out wonderfully fast. Watson with the Punjabi cavalry made a gallant charge, right into the enemy, turning them and capturing two of their guns, and Remmington's went right into the khets at them in most dashing style. Soon Pandy yielded. We did not know his strength and the crops were high, so we did not pursue fast enough. Remember our troops had just come in 31 miles, and were not quite fresh.

Everything naturally was in confusion. Major Ouvry even rode up to the 1st Troop and cheered them by saying that all our Punjab Cavalry had gone over to the enemy. I galloped to the right and found Younghusband had just made a charge and captured two guns, but had ridden horse and all, and his orderly horse and all, into a well. I brought up sappers and ropes and started them getting them out, and after a while, leaving some of the 8th and of his own men and sappers to go on with the work, I galloped on the Gwalior road and found the 3rd Europeans, in gorgeous scarlet, marching out, rather late if they really wanted any fire-eating: I passed them and found Infantry and guns halted, because some enclosures ahead were said to be full of Pandies: a queer reason for halting! Four Punjabis, a volunteer horseman and I went on a long way and found the enclosures quite empty, tho' some way ahead we saw their gharis going slowly off, and cavalry guarding them.

Our Cavalry and Horse Artillery, through fields on the left, were advancing, and soon they and the guns on the road galloped up and opened for a few rounds; then limbered up and pursued for a bit. This fire and pursuit was kept up, but as we had taken most of the guns and Pandy was flying, I should think pursuit alone was required, but the wearied Cavalry were not up for some time, and the pursuit was left almost to a few officers (Roberts, Norman and myself etc.).

Along the road (choked with camels, gharis, bundles etc.) and through the fields on either hand, were the flying enemy in hundreds − sepoys of 23rd, 22nd and 47th, 1st Cavalry, red-coated Irregulars, and men armed with matchlock and tulwar; they were so panic-struck that they let a few officers and (I suppose) Agra volunteers ride through them like sheep. It was absurd: excited as we were, we rode through them, slashing and thrusting, and leaving them behind. I knocked over lots, and killed 12 outright.

Some big Agra people (whom I knew not and whose orders I didn't much respect) were occasionally shouting for us to hold hard — rather difficult when Pandies swarmed in flight before us; strangely these men didn't resist: too anxious to escape, they didn't perceive how few we were, but of course thought numbers were at our backs; fresh cavalry up then would have killed thousands, whereas a few independent amateurs were doing butcher's work, for which privates are paid.

In the excitement I got quite foolhardy and, with the fugitives behind and on both sides of us, I still further detached myself to catch three red-coated sowars who with many others had made a turn to the left. I dashed off to intercept them and (as did they) saw too late my position. I was out of hail of anyone and the view at my back was of armed men in flight: the three sowars looked at me, exchanged glances and, still flying, drew together. I gathered my horse for a rush and, as it were, threw myself on the nearest. Before he thought I could be on him, I cut him down, and instantly turning on another saw him about ten paces off, firm as a rock, his carbine barrel steady and straight on me. I gave myself up for dead, but ducking my head instinctively, with my spurs in, I spun my horse round and round like a teetotum, the fiend still steady waiting for a sure shot. My horse stumbled and fell forward, and I too. The sowar fired simultaneously, missed me and was off again.

Oddly enough these armed men, so intent on flying, all gave me in my difficulties a wide berth, and neither cut at nor fired at me, or they

114

would have killed me easily, for no one saw me or was on my side of the road. There I was with Herat (the maneater who only one syce [groom] can hold and has to be muzzled and blinded), and there he was pulling away from me. However, he was pretty well done (I having ridden him without change from Hathras) and I managed to mount him and regain the road, and, some of our side coming up, I was all right again.

This was close to the Kari Nuddi, which the enemy crossed, fording it 10½ miles from Agra. We all pulled up as we reached the river and after a while the Horse Artillery came up and opened with ball on the enemy, as long as they were in sight. We rested by the river some time and then returned quietly. Being mounted and going as I liked, I was not in until past sunset, and the troops were not back until a good deal later.

We had taken heaps of luggage and 13 guns — all very good brass and very heavy metal. Were not we all done up! The 3rd Europeans thought they had done a fearful day's work, and (having marched only to the fifth milestone about) would ride on gun carriages etc. They look very fine fellows, very unruly, I expect, but good fighters: at present, however, they are griffs [newcomers], and don't know what work or fire means.

I don't know who commanded, I am sure. As usual I expect each Troop Captain and Cavalry Cornet did pretty well what seemed good to him. Greathed I saw frequently to the front, and men who had the air of Brigadiers and such like from Agra. Perhaps Greathed and Colonel Cotton [commanding troops at Agra], in conjunction, claim having fought the battle. The Infantry can't say that they had much to do and most certainly the 3rd Europeans had nothing to say to the fight, but looking very smart and strong and emptying the gharis along the road: the action was Cavalry and Artillery. The 75th behaved so much as usual that Gordon, who commands, actually said to me that they were so unsteady that he was beyond words disgusted with them.

11 October, Agra A quiet day spent in camp, recovering. Camp seems to afford great pleasure to the Agra people who come strolling about it, like Englishmen at Chobham. The volunteer Keranies bristle with swords, daggers and knives, even today, when all is quiet.

12 October, Agra Some of us rode from camp at daybreak to the Taj and I again saw that most perfect building with its lovely proportions, its pure white marble, exquisite carving and mosaics. Mrs Machell sang *'Mira! O Norma'* under the dome, but I think the echoes are too distracting. I drove back with Machells and Glovers to 'Buckingham Palace' and spent the day in Fort, breakfasting and dining with them.

Watts of our corps was there; he and I called on Colonel Fraser in his office and we gave him advice, abused the timid policy, and praised the Punjab most cheekily! He is a most jolly good old fellow, but his heroism as a man in the field contrasts strangely with his moral cowardice as ruler.

13 October, Agra Watts came down to camp and we walked up to the Fort. We saw how 6,000 Europeans and Eurasians were accommodated and quartered systematically in 'blocks' − such lots of women and children! − and how the Moti Masjid, that lovely little white mosque, was turned into a hospital, and Sisters of Mercy, 'Misses Nightingale', tended the sick beds.

That afternoon we went to a most jolly picnic at the Taj. The Taj was lighted up after dark with blue lights, and we dined on the floor of one of the side mosques, and danced on the smooth marble platform of the Taj to the music of Green's (2nd Punjab Infantry) band.

14 October, Agra Our camp was moved at daybreak across the river to the Mainpuri road, but I stayed behind and followed later at my leisure. Detachments from Delhi had come in. With them was Forbes of the Engineers, as a comrade for me: a very nice, quiet young fellow. I was very glad to see him.

He and I rode back to Agra in the afternoon and met the Ladies coming out to picnic at Rambagh (the fine native royal gardens on the Aligarh road). We joined them, had another very pleasant picnic, returned to 'Buckingham Palace', and sat up late playing round games. Forbes and I got beds in the Fort.

15 October, Etmadpur Forbes and I were obliged, at length, to say goodbye to the hospitalities and the civilisation of Agra and take again to our wanderings and campaigning; again let our beards grow and return to our khaki! We reached camp here at sunset. I heard of poor Salkeld's death; so now both the Victoria Cross officers are dead: and the *only* three officers attached to the 3rd Column (who passed through the Kashmere Gate) are the *only* officers in our corps who have died since the assault; Home, Salkeld and Tandy.

Elliot Brownlow writes in great distress at being obliged to remain at Delhi repairing the breaches, instead of campaigning. How I wish he would be sent to join this column! He made great friends with the future Mrs Lang, and eulogises her to my great satisfaction. I will send you his letter anent her.

As Monty would say, she is an 'awful stunner', the very nicest little girl ever born; and 'awfully' fond of me: she has never once missed sending me a long affectionate letter every day since I left Lahore. She likes Elliot Brownlow excessively, at which also I am delighted.

16 October, Firozabad We marched here — 14 miles — and I have letters by 2 mails to acknowledge, dated 10, 20 and 26 August. Very many thanks to all the kind contributors. The sad news from this wretched country gives the principal subject and tone to your letters; yet how your happy English life, your picnics and roamings, amidst lovely North Wales scenery, all the happiness of my dear home circle, contrasts with this life of war and confusion and anxiety. Yet I have nothing to complain of, everything to thank God for; much as I should long to be transported amongst you all again, I have really been very happy. Under the sad circumstances, I could not be happy in peace and quiet in England; I could not remain even at Lahore, under partial danger: I should, of course, have been burning to be employed as a man and a soldier in these stirring times, and I have enjoyed this new life which I have tried.

I have found that I really chose aright when I thought a soldier's life was the life for me. Exposure and fatigue, the music of ball and bullet, marching and roughing it, all that makes up a soldier's life, I enjoy. I am as happy as possible, and very thankful I ought to be that I have the disposition to bear an equal mind in these sorts of scenes, as well as for my preservation amongst so many great dangers: may I be spared yet to see all your dear faces again some day, when India has returned to peace; to her former state she never will.

'Delhi not fallen up to 27th June' disappointed you! What will you have said to continued disappointment up to the glorious 14th September, or more properly to 20th September. Even then what was the very great gain? Very much remains to be done; no revenge was taken then. I expect our loss was far greater than that of the enemy.

Our loss was 61 officers and 1,178 men in the assault alone — one third of the whole number engaged! Yet idiots in papers at home, who teach the multitude, themselves knowing Delhi as well as they do Peking or Mecca, say: 'What keeps our troops from taking a place with no fortifications, but only an old wall which a few pieces can batter down?' I wish the 'snub-nosed rogue from his counter and till', or his office stool, had had to charge a breach; he would not have called the high thick ramparts, the regular bastions, and deep ditches a mere nothing.

We ourselves rendered the defences of Delhi very strong and made bastions and Martello towers and glacis to them. And look at what the assault cost us: of all the Peninsular storms, Ciudad Rodrigo was hailed by the British nation as the proudest feat; yet Wellington took six times as many to the assault as we had at Delhi on the 14th, and lost fewer than we did. But the taking of Delhi can hardly be classed with sieges; the besieged so very greatly outnumbered the besiegers; the place could not be invested (as at Sebastopol) and (as at Sebastopol, too) the munitions of war of the besieged were limitless.

How pleasant to turn from thinking of this wretched country to your account of healthy walks and picnics amidst beautiful British scenery, all happy free peaceful Britain around you; how I would enjoy a breath of the free sea breezes, to smell the salt of the sea, and to see bold breakers dashing against the shore; to roam about English woods of beech and oak and pine, and along lanes of briar and honeysuckle – instead of these desolate plains peopled with cringing sinister-looking scoundrels, everything around impressed with rebellion and murder and treachery.

I am very glad that you think I only did my duty in volunteering for Delhi: it *was* my duty, and, except that you will have been doubly anxious on my account, I have every possible reason to rejoice that I was sent: I should have mourned all my life inaction at that crisis; now, if I am spared throughout, I shall look with delight and satisfaction at my *service*. I suppose I shall be 'under arms' for another year: for a regular war will be required for the resubjugation of Oudh: even now the papers urge our abandonment of Lucknow, important tho' it be to hold the capital of Oudh, and humiliating as it would seem to yield a foot before Pandy; yet as a military movement it would be better to concentrate at Cawnpore till such a force of British bayonets was assembled, that our progress should be certainly a perpetual victory, whereas the small force we could leave at Lucknow would be in perpetual danger.

18 October, Arowl Yesterday, another march of 14 miles brought us to Shikohabad; today a march of only 8 miles to Arowl, a small village.

Brigadier Grant came in today and took command of our column. He was Brigadier of Cavalry at Delhi – an active man, but not as young as Greathed. Greathed is made Brigadier of Infantry, and Ouvry of Cavalry to the Column. We heard that the Mainpuri Rajah was going to stand against us. A picket of his Cavalry was seen on the road in the morning by our advanced sowars.

19 October, Mainpuri Brigadier Grant took us a good march wherewith to commence his rule; he took us 23 miles, and as we started only at 2 a.m. we were not in till noon and the rearguard not till 4 p.m. The day being most intensely hot, I should think our European Infantry must have suffered; I know I did, and I was afraid I was going to have one of my pleasant fever attacks. However, I think I shall get all right, having gone on the sick list yesterday.

This Mainpuri seems a very pretty station, tho' now of course ruined and neglected. The church, though not pretty, is English-looking and paths lead to it through what is now a tangled wilderness of shrubs and flowers.

The young Rajah and his men have fled; his uncle met us yesterday on the road: he is a rival of his nephew's and tells us all sorts of stories against him. In the Fort are about 12,000 lbs of native powder, and a gun foundry: a gun being made, the bricks about it still hot, has been found. Brigadier Grant has ordered this Fort to be destroyed and the Sappers have been at work up there all day, and are going to blow a great part of it to bits this evening.

I forgot to say that Major Macleod of our corps joined us at Agra, and so I ceased to be Engineer No.1. He seems a very nice pleasant man. This sort of marching is tiring work. One is fit for but little writing during the day, but feels stupid and sleepy.

22 October, Gooshahi Ganj In the evening of 20 October we got orders to leave the Sappers behind to destroy Mainpuri Fort: they could not do it on the 20th, as all day property was being taken out of the Fort and treasure counted there: of course this was the fault of the civilians. We are burdened always with one or more civilians who hamper our every movement, save every Pandy they can, and try and claim all loot as theirs. The North-Wester (you're retired, Father,) is a regular Cutcherry party [Courthouse man] who half despises, half dreads, and altogether hates the 'brutal and lawless soldiery'. While protected by their strong arm he comes back to the districts he could not keep in order before, hails with delight his cringing scoundrels of omlahs [clerks] and, ignoring their having been in rebellion, probably robbing and murdering the Firinghis [Europeans] for many months, claims immunity for them and puts the poor fellows into tahsils and such like appointments.

The Mainpuri Rajah having bolted, of course his uncle, by flattering and grovelling, is instantly appointed Tahsildar of Mainpuri. Cocks [Sessions judge at Mainpuri] tried to save the Fort for his residence and so delayed removal of two lakhs [200,000 Rupees] of treasure, so that they were not in our camp until 1 at night. However, Cocks and the Rajah's uncle were sold and the latter had the pleasure of seeing the place in which he had promised himself a snug residence blown to bits.

Being seedy, I did not stay with the Sappers, and tracked in a doolie with the column. We made a 14 mile march to Bewar. The Sappers did not come in till 4 pm, poor fellows, and we suddenly got orders to march all night to Gooshahi Ganj: 29 miles. The order came so late that I could not get a doolie. Consequently, what with the long march when I was ill, and the sleeping during the halt under the heavy dew, and the scorching sun in the morning (for it was so well managed that with our starting at 8 at night our halts were so long that we did not get in till 11), I was very ill and thought I had sunstroke; however, lots of leeches last night brought me round, and as I made the march this morning (13 miles) in a doolie I am much better today.

23 October, Meerum Serai Here we are little more than 50 miles from Cawnpore, at which place I expect we shall be in three days' time, as a cossid came in this morning with a little note (written in Greek character) from Cawnpore to urge immediate advance as provisions at Lucknow could not last beyond the 10 Nov. The fighting column will be at the final and real relief of Lucknow.

I had the pleasure (as I lay in a doolie) to hear the guns going away to the left in the direction of the Kali Nadi. It appears that an escort of sowars (15th Irregulars) came down from Fatehgarh to bring in four guns (three English 24-pr howitzers and one 6-pr) and two native. Roberts, hearing of it as he rode on, went down towards the river and saw them crossing, and sent to Ouvry for two Horse Artillery guns and cavalry. Up they came and took the four guns, and the cavalry (Probyn and Watson) went in pursuit; three risaldars [Indian cavalry officers] among them were killed, one carrying a woman behind him. Roberts had his horse badly slashed and came back on a captured native tat with native trappings. Young Mackenzie (of the 8th Lt Cavalry) slashing at a man, missed him, and cut through his own boot and foot rather badly. He must have dropped his eyeglass.

Grant I believe intends doing the remaining 50 odd miles to Cawnpore in three marches, and then will go the picked Delhi Khakis and the new English regiments to the real relief of Lucknow, and we can manage that long before the latest safe date (10 Nov). I don't think our Greek correspondent from Cawnpore thinks we are so near. When we get there we will really know how many English troops have come up, and who were found alive and safe at Lucknow.

28 October, Cawnpore Here we are, and have been for two days and more, at the most tragical spot in the history of this rebellion.

On the 26th we came in very proudly, bands playing. In the evening and yesterday morning I paid visits to the scene of poor Wheeler's defence and that fiend the Nana Sahib's atrocities.

There is a little house, near the Assembly Rooms and the old Hotel, on the road between them, a low tiled-roof house, built in Pompeian style, around an open central courtyard. In that courtyard stood a tree, where English ladies were hanging when Neill's troops marched in; it is cut down now. In every room of that little house, on floor and walls, are stains of blood, and on the walls hundreds of bullet marks; even now remain stray socks, slippers and bits of clothing. When Neill's soldiers entered, the place was heaped with clothing of women and children.

In the compound stands a tree, marked with bullet holes and sword gashes; in the latter is still long hair; amongst the grass and bushes of the compound, between the house and well, are still strips of clothing and locks of long hair; into that well upwards of 200 bodies of women and children were thrown, many still alive. No one who has seen that spot can ever feel anything but deep hatred to the Nana and his fellow fiends and all his fellow race. No officer standing in those rooms spoke to another, tho' each knew his neighbour's feelings. I know I could not have spoken. I felt as if my heart was stone and my brain fire, and that the spot was enough to drive one mad. Neill made his high-caste Brahmin and Mussalman sepoy prisoners lick the stains on the floor and wall before he hung them. The gallows on which he hung them is the only pleasant thing in the compound on which to rest the eye.

All these fiends will never be repaid one-tenth of what they deserve; many a man will cringe before us and serve us well and faithfully! (the brutes), who will secretly chuckle in his black heart in having abetted in these scenes. Every man across the river whom I meet shall suffer for my visit to Cawnpore. I will never again, as I used to at Delhi, let off men, whom I catch in houses or elsewhere. I thought when I had killed twelve men outright and wounded or knocked over as many more at the battle of Agra, that I had done enough: I think now I shall never stop, if I get a chance again.

We also visited the scene of poor Wheeler's defence. Such a place! you would say no one could have held out in such a position for two days or even one! The fact is Wheeler never believed he would have to defend it; he summoned together all the Europeans, so as to have them together; he never believed that the sepoys would attack him, and he believed Lord Canning's *promise* that if he only held out, he should be relieved on a certain date; that certain date was a *fortnight* before the date on which Wheeler capitulated. Wheeler, trusting in Lord Canning's *word*, would not let the officers send the Ladies away when they could have done so! Had Wheeler really thought that he would have had to stand a siege, he would of course have held some post on the river bank, where under the high cliffs the Ladies would have been quite safe, and where they could have eventually taken refuge in boats. As it was, this is the position:-

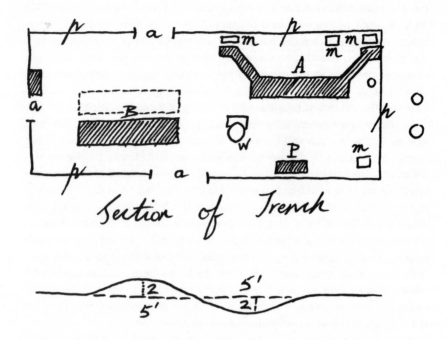

WHEELER'S LAST STAND – as sketched by A.M. Lang in October 1857

A. and B. are two pukka barracks, with a great deal of open parade on all sides, but on one, unfortunately, are new barracks being built, the nearest of which are very near. W. is the pukka well, completely exposed, its *chabutra* [seating platform] smashed to pieces, showing how it was a special mark for the enemy. P. is a small picket-house: m.m. etc. are earthen magazines made by the defenders. The line round, p.p.p., represents the trench!! – see the section. What a mockery to call it an entrenchment: were you to ride over it in the dark you would not perceive it!

The roof of A. was fired by carcasses [incendiary shells] and fell in, and then fancy poor delicate Ladies and little children lying out, day and night, in that trench in June, with those curs barking round them, not daring to charge that little devoted band. In a few places, a.a.a., the trench is discontinued. Those are the batteries! At least, there in the open stood our guns (eight 9-prs and one 24-pr howitzer); out of 8 officers, 67 men, and 9 guns, only 2 officers, 12 men and 2 guns were existing at the capitulation.

The buildings themselves: never did I see buildings so thoroughly riddled — not a foot unscarred by round shot; you would wonder how any hardy soldiers could have held them for two days, much less that delicate women and children could have lived through 22 days of siege. Of course barracks have ordinary walls, through which 18-pr balls would crash with ease.

Low down on one wall is the scar of a ball; all round it the blood, and brains and hair of young Wheeler, who lying on the floor wounded, his sister kneeling over and fanning him, was killed by this ball. Within sight of these two barracks, round which the Nana Sahib and his followers settled themselves to testing from a distance that little English band, stands the asylum built for the orphans during the last great famine. Every heart and purse will be closed now, I fancy, should another famine come.

The floors are still covered with mementoes of the defenders; a sock, a child's shoe, letters, leaves of books, pieces of music, papers, etc. One officer picked up Wheeler's last pay certificate; another a few leaves of a book bearing the name of a Lady whom he well knew; another letters of a great friend of his, and so on; it was very sad work looking at all this, and more than sad. I felt that I could vow my life to revenge, to take blood from that race every day, to tear all pity from one's heart. I would not go there again for anything.

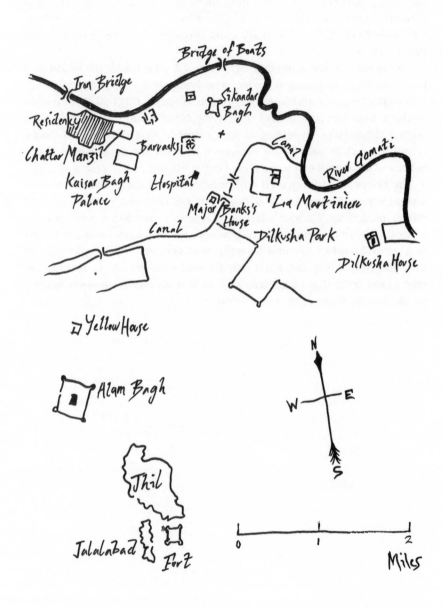

THE APPROACH TO LUCKNOW, NOVEMBER 1857

124

CHAPTER 10

On To Lucknow

For the column, the march from Cawnpore to Lucknow was not just another few miles of marching and fighting; it was a journey into a different world. The kingdom of Oudh had only recently been annexed by the British, and this annexation had been nothing like that of the Punjab. The British had moved in because the appalling corruption of the royal administration had exploited the poorest in the land, but in this case even those who benefited from Sir Henry Lawrence's reforms had not welcomed them. Oudh resented the British. Here the Mutiny was not just a matter for the sepoys; it was supported by the majority of the population.

Even so, the focus of rebellion was as elsewhere in the cities rather than the countryside, primarily in the capital city of Lucknow. Here the British had been holding out in the grounds of the Residency, first under Sir Henry Lawrence himself, and now under those who had led the first relief, Havelock and Lawrence's successor, General Sir James Outram. Knowing that Sir Colin Campbell was on his way, Outram smuggled out to him advice on how best to make his advance on Lucknow. By chance Lang was to be there when Sir Colin took his decision to follow that advice, and for once he saw a Chief Engineer's plan rejected.

31 October, Bashiratganj At last we have taken the field again and left Cawnpore, and are fairly in 'Pandy-land', in Oudh, which is really enemy's country, all the people being openly against us.

The 27th, 28th, 29th and 30th we spent lazily, recruiting strength at Cawnpore. Only one of our corps did we find there, Watson. He comes on with us to Lucknow. I find him a very fine fellow. He was with Havelock in 3 or 4 battles between this and Lucknow, but was not with him when he fought his way to the Residency. Since he left this place Havelock has 69 officers killed and wounded, and about 1000 men. The proportion of killed to wounded is excessive, nearly half.

As to the Nana Sahib, some say he is only about 20 miles off, in Oudh, while others say he has gone to Kalpi to take charge of the Gwalior and Indore rebels, who with a heavy siege-train are crossing at that place.

At Cawnpore we collected as much as the hurry would allow us, fascines, sandbags, etc. to take on to Lucknow. The whole Engineer Brigade from Delhi expected to have joined us, but at 2 this morning we started off for this place, three or four miles on the Lucknow side of Unnao.

We expect three officers and 100 men of the Royal Engineers to be up presently, and ditto of the Madras Engineers and Sappers, but all these are late. We have not England to thank for the taking of Delhi, or saving of Agra, and as to the relief of Lucknow, the Punjab troops and those stopped from the 'China' force alone will have anything to say to it. Not a soldier sent from England for the saving of India will arrive before all the great deeds have been completely done, without their assistance.

This Bashiratganj is like a long street or narrow serai, the shops or compartments opening on to the road, and a gateway closing each end, just such a place as Pandy would love to defend. Havelock fought four battles here, falling back after each one to Cawnpore. We have seen no one, not even a villager, on our march so far as this. Our force is diminished by two Horse Artillery guns, a squadron of Lancers, and the 5th Punjab Cavalry, who have stayed behind at Cawnpore to form an escort for Sir Colin Campbell, but we have brought on with us four companies of the 93rd, 150 of the 5th Fusiliers, and 70 of the 53rd, and 3 officers and 60 men of the Royal Artillery to whom have been made over the heavy guns of our column (two 18-pounder guns and two 8-inch howitzers).

I was talking to a young Royal Artillery officer this morning: he was just from the Cape, and the Artillery, having never before been in India, are griffs as to it. His style was very amusing, opening with 'I suppose you have some pleasant stations up in the interior.'

The 93rd are the boys; such glorious thoro' Highlanders and Scots: the pipes are delicious, so thoroughly British, recalling the 78th Pipes at Chatham Lines, or this very regiment, or the 42nd, at Chobham. I should not mind where I was ordered with these fellows behind me. They are called the Wilayati [British] Gurkhas, with legs like young elephants. They wear their kilts and sporran all complete, a loose smock tunic, khaki with red cuffs and collar, and their feather bonnets with a white puggree round the lower part of them. It was so jolly to watch them march through the Pandy port of Bashiratganj with their Highland pipes screaming. The Punjabis fraternize with them mostly, and delight in the pipes. As I walked home from mess last night after the pipers had finished playing, I found knots of mingled Hielanders and Sikhs and Afghans, each jabbering away in his own language, not in the least understood by one another, but great friends, one going on 'Weel, weel', and 'Hoot mon', and the other 'Hamne Matadeenko khub mara' [I killed lots of Mata Deens] and so on: a great shaven-headed Pathan would be trying on a Hieland bonnet!

1 November, Newalganj Started at 3 and marched about 14 miles here, one mile from the Lucknow side of the River Sai. The Sai is twelve miles from Lucknow. It is crossed by a bridge of seven arches; of these arches the large centre one was broken, leaving a span of twenty or twenty-four feet to bridge. Luckily on the left was a good ford, over which our troops, guns and baggage were the whole day crossing.

We Engineer officers spent the whole day at the river, making firm ghats to the ford, the sappers bringing large thatch roofs from the village on the bank and laying them down on the ghat. We also got the longest timbers we could from the village and threw a foot-traffic rough bridge across the broken span. All day we heard the booming of the Lucknow guns.

2 November, Banthra At 7 o'clock in the morning we marched from Newalganj to move our camp to this village, about three miles. As usual, Roberts and Mayne [Assistant Quartermaster Generals], as soon as they caught sight of the village of the destined camping ground, galloped ahead; they spoke to one or two villagers asking for information, but got but few rough answers, and suddenly a rush of musket and matchlock men was made from the village. Off they galloped for their lines, having to take a circuitous route through the fields round the village, to rejoin the advanced guard. Roberts's horse was hit and fell over him (Roberts getting his thumb cut), but luckily he was unhurt, remounted and got safely back.

The advanced guard went ahead, two guns (supported by a squadron of Lancers, and Watson's and Probyn's Punjab Cavalry) opened from the road on the village. The 75th and Sappers advanced skirmishing through the fields on the left towards the village. The enemy kept up a most steady fire, out of range!

The 75th and Sappers cleared the village (as they thought), the latter losing two killed and five wounded (one mortally). The former of course went round outside, and lost none. On they went and the two guns

127

continued along the road, supported by Lancers and Probyn. Watson and his men galloped ahead on the right; the rest of the Artillery had galloped up through the fields, and the Infantry and 93rd Highlanders, 5th, 53rd, etc. also were coming up as fast as they could. I did not see them fight, but Banthra, which the 75th and Sappers had left in the rear, occupied the main column some two hours; the Royal Artillery came up with an 18-pounder (Horse Artillery fashion) and opened on the village: some sixty men were killed in the village, the 93rd losing one killed, and two or three wounded, and an officer severely wounded. Wilde's Corps lost five wounded and Green, two. However, I saw none of this, as I joined Watson's Cavalry; he gave pursuit with his whole regiment thro' a jhil and here some fourteen were caught and killed. It was a picturesque sight seeing the Irregulars splashing through the great jhil, and really one saw what one reads about the 'waters being crimsoned with blood'.

Watson pursued for a mile beyond the jhil, but we only caught a few men and had to pull up by a village, from which about a hundred footmen ran out, and advancing thro' the khets sent their bullets whizzing about us; a body of cavalry began to move slowly towards us from the front and a few appeared in our rear; on which we had 'threes about' and retreated at a gallop, or 'bolted'.

We found the Artillery, Lancers and Highlanders about a mile in our rear, and there, a line of battle being formed, we advanced again, the Horse Artillery and Cavalry going forward at the gallop, and, after advancing about a mile or more, opened fire. The enemy answered from two or three guns, one of which we took − an old injured 9-pounder, which had been mended and furnished with a great ugly muzzle.

We stopped at about 2 o'clock, having been engaged since 8, pursuing a perpetually bolting enemy, whose numbers I am sure no one can affirm from actual eyesight to have exceeded 150 sowars and the same number of footmen, tho' of course many declare, arguing from probabilities, that there must have been 1,000 or more. Anyhow, no one was satisfied that our men should have been so knocked about for so little a result.

When we had marched between four and five miles beyond Banthra and were within four miles of Alam Bagh, we were marched *back* to Banthra! (Why, no one knows, for we have here a bad encamping ground; ahead there are splendid level plains, with pukka wells). About six or eight villages were burned and are still burning. A bhisti [water carrier] went just now to a village to draw water and had his nose, ears and hands cut off, so the scoundrels linger about us still.

3 November, Banthra Halted here. The enemy seem to have cavalry moving all round us, as the various outlying pickets have in turn been firing volleys of musketry. We shall again have to fight over ground we held yesterday! Of course we know nothing of Sir Colin; the road behind us is closed. We hear the Lucknow guns, but there is but little firing.

6 November, Banthra Here we are halting in the most provoking manner, because we mustn't attack without Sir Colin. Yesterday 1,500 men and 6 guns convoyed ammunition and provisions to Alam Bagh — Macleod would not let me go. The Lancers and Irregulars and Harrington with two guns were completely routed by hornets! Harrington, severely stung, was very ill at night from the effects. The party who came back from Alam Bagh last night describe it as large enclosure, 500 yards by 470 yards, rectangular, with a two-storied gilded domed tower at each of the four corners; a large double-storied bara dari [reception hall] in the centre; a gateway in the centre of each side — the principal one, towards the roads, having a building on each side of the entrance. A wall 11 feet high and 2½ feet thick encloses it. Since our occupation of it, a ditch has been dug round it on the outside, and the earth heaped against the walls; a banquette of earth has been raised on the interior side and the wall has been loopholed.

All round the place is an open plain for 800 yards and upwards. The man in command there, Major Colin Campbell McIntyre, will allow no one to go outside. Were he to throw up an earthwork, or establish a picket 4, 5, or even 800 yards off, he could hold all that extra ground, and the men could get fresh air and exercise. As it is, the atmosphere of that place, where they have been shut up with hundreds of camels, bullocks and elephants, tells on the men and they look pale and sickly, so they say. A gun, about 1,000 yards off on their left front, pitches 6-pounder balls up towards the gateway, but all this time only three coolies have been hit. This gun the commandant will not attempt to take, for fear of losing a man. He has 1,100 European Infantry with him. He puts no end of officers under arrest — eight on one day for going outside to have a little practice with rifles at Pandy! Judge, of the Engineers, is perpetually threatened with arrest and only spared because he is the only officer of Engineers there.

I wonder that we are not all marched there and encamped on that fine open plain.

Today a convoy takes thousands of camels, elephants and carts back to Cawnpore, so my letter will be taken all right. Sir Colin is at Cawnpore. He has made Major Goodwyn of our Corps his Chief Engineer, thus ousting poor Major Macleod who goes back with the convoy. I am very sorry indeed for this, as Major Macleod is the most pleasant of commanding officers, and a very clear-headed far-seeing officer. Watson is to be Brigade Major of Engineers.

8 November, Banthra At about 2 p.m. yesterday arrived a reinforcement of 400 of the 93rd, 150 of 53rd, and 100 sailors of the *Shannon* with four 24-pounders. It was grand to see Jack Tars again, with their loose open large-collared blue shirts, loose blue trousers, straw hats with white covers, black ribbands and 'Shannon' on their bands; they carry musket and bayonet. They seem so strange and out of place, rolling about up here, using their sea-language among the niggers, driving bullock gharis and swearing because 'she tacks about and backs and fills so'. I don't know what the Hindustanis think of them.

We have some jumping and hopping by way of exercise in this stupid halting place. Then at 3½ p.m. we received orders to march back to the [River] Sai and make good approaches to the river banks; so Watson, Forbes, Stevenson and I, with the Sappers, marched back four miles and stayed till the ghats were all smooth. This was a change and as such pleasant, and our ordinary mess dinner was agreeably exchanged for an al fresco feast of cold meat and bread on the Bridge of Sighs.

Just before sunset appeared my young friend Charlie Hunter of the Horse Artillery who had galloped down to bring to Watson and me the first letters we have seen since leaving Cawnpore. You may imagine how sappers and timbers and the broken arch and the still Sai, India generally and the wretched country all about us, were forgotten as we sat on the bridge parapet, and were at once transported to other happier scenes.

Today we have a quiet Sunday and have had a comfortable service for the officers in the large mess tent of the Lancers. Sadly, I don't think it a good religious school, a camp; nor do I see any more serious living induced by the extra danger, nor does common danger seem to draw men nearer to one another.

I don't think that religion or a feeling of the uncertainties of life, or of man's nothingness are fostered by the dangers of warfare. On the contrary, on minds constituted as mine is, they have the opposite effect. They cause elation of spirits, scorn of danger, an inclination of confidence in pluck and strength, and a sort of feeling of *self*-satisfaction in escaping unhurt.

I had thought it would be different: there is nothing like danger from pestilence (like the cholera at Mian Mir last year) to bring a man to feel his real position. So on the whole I don't think campaigning good for a man, or I should say for my own special case.

As to how my spirits and health fare, both are first rate. Though not

COLIN CAMPBELL (1792-1863)

Campbell may now seem an exception to the rule of Victorian Britain: a carpenter's son, he became Field-Marshal. In fact, others too rose rapidly. He served with Wellington in Spain, soldiered in India, commanded a division in the Crimea. Though personally brave, he was nicknamed Sir Crawling Camel, known less for dash than for care of his troops. Lang liked him on first acquaintance and admired his Relief of Lucknow, during which Campbell promised him a VC. Subsequently, however, his caution irritated the Delhi veterans, and prolonged the conflict.

so fine a climate by any manner of means as the Punjab — and camp life *before the enemy* (for one cannot wander about and shoot etc.) does not do a man the same good as cold weather hunting and cricket and such-like occupations of peaceful days — yet the cold weather is setting the whole army up, and good beef and beer (as several of our well-fed messes still boast) and the climate are making us pick up strength and flesh and muscle again. It will I hope completely overcome any ill-effects that must be induced by that Delhi campaigning. Very very many will have cause to remember Delhi, who escaped wounds there, yet had their constitutions more or less affected for life — and many of my friends are among them.

I have as yet been most mercifully preserved, more so than most officers; for I have outlasted more dangerous duties and seen more actual danger than perhaps any of them here. At Delhi I seemed to myself to have a sort of charmed life, and latterly, when under no excitement it cost no effort of courage to face any amount of fire. I find that the music of round shot and bullet, the roar of artillery etc. all quicken my life as it were, and exhilarate me exceedingly; and so I rejoice in being a soldier and seeing service.

Sir Colin we expect tomorrow.

11 November, Banthra On 9 November, at 4 p.m., came in Sir Colin Campbell and his staff, and the escort whom we had left for him. On 10 November Major Goodwyn came into camp, as Chief Engineer.

I was in bed at 9 p.m. and up at 11 p.m., roused by Goodwyn. Shivering in our cold tent, niggers driven away from earshot of our secrets, we were initiated into the mysteries of G's plans of attack. Then soon after daybreak Sir Colin and General Mansfield came into my tent and found us at our task, copying plans and writing. He swept away the plan of Goodwyn, and declared that he would adhere to Outram's instructions. Goodwyn tried hard to urge his plan, and at last Sir C.C. got regularly riled and told him that he had borne with him for two days, and now he would not hear another word.

Sir Colin impressed me most favourably on first sight: most jolly, impetuous and energetic; intensely impulsive and warm, when roused — and that is pretty often, I expect. He looked a 'character' as he stood, with both hands gesticulating and hissing through clenched teeth how he would carry out those plans. General Mansfield seems a neat, gentlemanly, quiet, courteous officer, and, I should think, shrewd and clear-sighted.

We worked at writing out Outram's directions. I have just done you a rough little plan of Lucknow, showing the buildings likely to be interesting for the operations of the next few days [see page 124] Of course, I may not write down the plans of operations as we are bound to secrecy; besides this letter may find its way into enemy's hands. All I know is that I wish the affair was over. I think we shall only relieve the garrison of Lucknow and then abandon Oudh, go on and thrash the Gwalior troops who in very great strength are threatening the Doab. The reconquest of Oudh will be deferred until we have an overwhelming army.

I hope this mail will take home the happy news of the liberation of Outram and Havelock and all the Ladies and children. It is the pretty fair sex whose presence in this country has made this such a dreadful war. Three have been killed by round shot in the Residency. Fancy Ladies suffering such a fate. Please God our army will bring them out all safe.

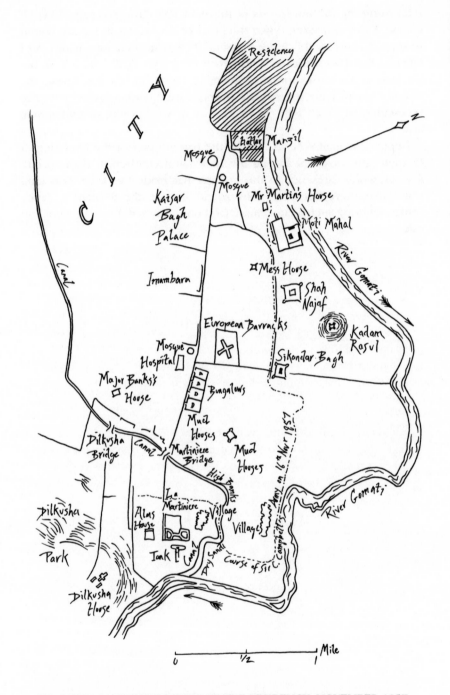

SIR COLIN CAMPBELL'S RELIEF OF THE RESIDENCY, NOVEMBER 1857

CHAPTER 11

Lucknow Relieved

Sir Colin Campbell was to be sharply criticized later for some of his decisions as Commander-in-Chief, not least by Lang, but there is no doubt that his relief of Lucknow in November, 1857, was a brilliant feat. Although hugely outnumbered, with 8,000 troops against some 100,000, he managed not only to reach the Residency at remarkably little cost, but also to bring out the sick, the women and children quite unharmed. For Lang, Sir Colin's success was a matter for personal as well as military concern. His first cousin, Walter Freeling, was a number of Havelock's force.

Unlike Delhi, Lucknow had no wall, and the route Campbell chose was that recommended by Outram — through the suburbs and back streets of the city. He was magnificently served by as heterogeneous a force as could be imagined, with Sikhs and Highlanders, Gurkhas and even the Royal Navy fighting side by side. It has to be remembered too that it was not an easy force to weld into an effective war machine. There was considerable tension between those who had spent all their army careers in India and those who had now been sent from Britain to sort out what they saw as a mess caused by the Indian Army. It was especially hard for young veterans of Delhi, such as Lang, to welcome the arrival of older, more senior, but less battle-hardened officers. The success of this army was due not simply to good generalship, but to a remarkable willingness of all the participants to lay aside their own differences in the face of what seemed an almost overwhelming foe.

12 November, Alam Bagh, near Lucknow At 7 we marched for Alam Bagh, and had a fight with the enemy at Jalalabad on the right of the road. We captured the two guns they brought out to fight us in the open.

They were caught in retreat by Gough and his Plungers stuck in a jhil, and there some twenty of the enemy were cut up in the water. Some fought splendidly: one magnificent man stood at bay in the jhil; Gough went at him, but got for his pains a slash on the head which nearly knocked him off his horse, and cut his puggree (which certainly saved his life) and a slash of his pet horse. A sowar went at him, but Pandy caught the tulwar in his hand, got it, and with two tulwars kept a lot at bay till a fellow with an immensely long lance speared him.

We did not get in till past twelve. Then, as soon as we had pitched tents, some round shots coming in, we had to move camp about 300 yards back.

We started a semaphore on the top of one of the corner towers of Alam Bagh, and from the top of the Chattar Manzil in Lucknow Outram replied, and they talked all day.

14 November, At Lucknow Yesterday Brigadier Hope and a column marched on Jalalabad and found it deserted save by monkeys! Today, all the tents and superfluous baggage having been sent into Alam Bagh, and the 75th left as a garrison; the army commenced its march after the men had breakfasted. We had about 3,200 Infantry and 700 Cavalry.

We marched to the north-east, across country, crossing the Jalalabad road and going in the direction of the south-eastern corner of the Dilkusha Park. We saw hardly any enemy and advanced leisurely, the advanced guard often halting so that the heavy guns with the main column might keep up. At last appeared the village of Bibiapur, and beyond over broken ground, the stone wall of Dilkusha Park. Crash went our six-pounder balls onto Bibiapur; out went our skirmishers, but the few Pandies vanished, and on we went to where the high gilded roof of Dilkusha rose above the trees.

Such a pretty scene it was: the park about the King's Shooting House of a Palace, the broken ground, and dotted deer, the blue winding Gomati gleaming here and there beyond, the beautiful black buck and antelope bounding along and looking startled at our advance, the lazy nilgai [short-horned antelope] shambling off disgusted at being disturbed − a scene all fitted for peace, and quite profaned by the appearance of a Lancer officer and Lt Lang riding cautiously towards the house, peering beyond the trees and outhouses, with finger on the pistol trigger and spur ready on horse's flank.

Seeing no one about the house, the Lancer officer rode back to report the place empty; but I thought I saw a man come out of an outhouse. Followed at a distance by Watson, I rode almost up to the steps of the house, when I heard Watson shout to me to come back, and back I galloped as hard as I could, just in time, for some men had come rushing up, from whence I don't know, and ping ping came a shower of bullets. Sir Colin and the staff, who were outside, rushed to the shelter of the wall, and infantry were sent skirmishing into the pretty park to the dismay of the antelope. Some of our men fired at what they thought were Pandies in the trees, but what turned out to be monkeys!

Meanwhile the Sappers were levelling a bit of wall and in came the Artillery. Dilkusha House being taken, the force threw right shoulders forward and through the trees and down the hill towards the Martinière came the infantry skirmishing, and other guns supported by cavalry.

Our men were suffering but very little and the opposition was very slight. Soon after our heavy guns had come up on the high ground and opened on the Martinière, the enemy abandoned the grand big building, and I rode my horse up the broad steps into the house, and was first into the empty place, for which I was seized on by Major Goodwyn to stay there and hold it with some sappers, as the others passed beyond.

Mounting up the *seven* stories up to the top, I had a beautiful lookout and could see the direction our troops took on the left, going straight at the canal by Banks's House, the Dilkusha bridge and the Martinière bridge (the first broken, the second broken and made a dam, by which the lower part of the canal became only a sandy channel.) On the right I saw Watson and Probyn cross the sandy channel and, turning between the River Gomati and the village there, charge the enemy's cavalry. Watson fought like a 'lion' as his men said: his steel gauntlet was cut through at the knuckles, he was nearly stunned by a cut on the head, which his puggree saved from being fatal; his arm and leg were both hit and bruised, and how he escaped in the crowd of enemy he was amongst seemed a miracle.

That evening we held Dilkusha and the Martinière, the latter an immense building, as big as Greenwich Hospital: the former, tho' much smaller, from its very commanding position on the high ground of the Park, the best military post: the Chief and his staff, and the Engineers with their park etc., were in the Martinière: the troops were bivouacked in the Park and about the Martinière, and our pickets were out near the canal on right, centre, and left, and our mortars played away all night over Banks's House.

15 November In the morning I was with some other officers and sappers making a road down to and across the canal, where the banks are quite low and the channel simply a sandy road. In the afternoon the enemy came out: cavalry, infantry, and two guns. Probyn and Watson being by the Martinière tank [lake] moved forward; the enemy's first shot went straight into a small reconnoitring party and knocked over a horse and sowar. Up came the two Madras Horse Artillery guns and opened from our side of the canal: then up came more guns, Remmington's Troop, and over they went with the Cavalry, on which off went the enemy just the same route as the evening before, and got away their guns: however, *as usual*, heaps of ammunition was thrown away, as nearly all Light Artillery and Cavalry and some Infantry were out blazing away for an hour or more, on account of this irritating little move of Pandy's.

We had a semaphore raised on the Martinière top to talk to the Chattar Manzil during the day. We had a beautiful view over the buildings of Lucknow from the Martinière, forests of domes, minarets, and gilded pinnacles, stretching away as far as the eye could see, that wonderful river, the Gomati, appearing everywhere in the most impossible twisting manner, but *the* sight was the glorious British Union Jack flying at the Chattar Manzil.

Major Goodwyn drew down the odium of all our corps by resigning his appointment in a huff: so a Lt Lennox of *Royal* Engineers (hang them all, what do they mean by coming here) is our Chief Engineer: a very pleasant fellow, but fancy an R.E. Lt Chief Engineer in an army in Bengal!

16 November After breakfast the troops again advanced: we had left all our camels and baggage at the Dilkusha and each of us carried three days' provisions only. I was in the advanced guard with some sappers. We marched at the back of the Martinière, into the canal, then down the channel, till we were close to the Gomati, and along the Gomati banks for some way; then through fields and mango topes [groves] and, *single file*, through the narrowest of little paths, buried in huts and trees (such a place! if Pandy had only caught us there!) into a street of mud houses, a Lucknow suburb (Sultan Ganj). But we had turned Pandy's flank and he had not expected us there.

Then began our work, some of our sappers knocking down a mud wall so that a big 24-pounder might play from the street at the Sikandar Bagh, an enclosed garden held by 2000 Pandies. Then we were at work in making ramps from the street up some banks, up which we pulled more heavy guns, and in a little time we had several heavy guns and some light guns smashing away at the Sikandar Bagh, infantry lying under shelter ready for a rush, and some dragging away at the ropes of the heavy guns, bringing them into position, Pandy all the while keeping up no end of a fire from the walls of Sikandar Bagh.

While I was working hard at getting one of these guns dragged close up, I saw Lt Paul rush ahead waving his sword, and the 4th Punjabis yelling and shouting, as they charged along behind him straight at the building. The effect was electrical; down we dropped the ropes and rushed along too; up sprung 93rd and 53rd and, cheering and shouting 'Remember Cawnpore', on we went, some at a breach in one of the corner towers and some (with whom I was) over a loopholed mud wall straight at the gate; axes and muskets soon smashed in the gate, and then didn't we get revenge − the first good revenge I have seen!

Such a distracting row of thousands of rifles firing without intermission I never heard, and such a sight of slaughter I never saw. In the open rooms right and left of the archway Pandies were shot down and bayoneted in heaps, three or four feet deep; in the centre Bara Dari they made but little stand, but at the house in the middle of the rear wall and in the semicircular court beyond it they shut the many thin doors and thousands of bullets were poured in, into the masses. It was a glorious sight to see the mass of bodies, dead and wounded, when we did get in. The bodies have now been buried and counted − 1,840 Pandies.

The mass of bodies were set fire to, and to hear the living as they caught fire calling out in agony to be shot was horrible even in that scene where all men's worst passions were excited; but remember that our men and officers were still being hit; at each corner tower a few desperate men were holding out, and lives were being thrown away in attempting to force little narrow winding staircases where men were determined to hold out as long as possible. I had a muzzle at my chest, the hand which held the stock I couldn't see, and back I sprang, you may be certain. That same man held out for two hours up his staircase, and when his ammunition was done, appeared on the roof at top, and with fury, hurled his tulwar down amongst us, and fell amongst a volley of bullets.

Sixty or more were taken alive and put up in a line, and they got no mercy, being caught when our fellows' blood was so much up; they got kicked and spit at and pricked with swords, and always with 'Cawnpore, you scoundrels', and then they were all shot: a great many were 1st N.I., *the* bad regiment at Cawnpore.

I was told to remain with sappers in Sikandar Bagh, and was there three hours. Yet when I left the place was not yet thoroughly ours, and we had lost many officers and men. I was hit, for the first time, by a bullet but was unwounded most fortunately: I was sent spinning by a stinging crack on the shoulder, with my sword flying out of my hand. I thought I was killed, but I was highly delighted when I found I didn't drop, and a man called out that the bullet had hit the wall beyond me. It was a sharp glance off my pouch-belt, and the only effect was to make my shoulder and arm bruised and stiff for a couple of days. But many poor fellows were killed: all the 4th Punjabi officers were hit; poor Paul, who behaved splendidly, was blown up, or rather burned up, by an explosion. Young Benson, a Civil Service volunteer who had accompanied our force to meet his brother in Lucknow, was shot in trying one of these towers and is dead.

When I was ordered on from Sikandar Bagh with some Madras Sappers, I heard that two or three companies of the 93rd had gone up the straight road to the European Barracks, and taken them; that on the right Green's 2nd Punjabis had taken Kadam Rasul (unopposed), and that for the rest my eyes showed me the state of affairs, i.e. our guns, heavy and light, were playing away on the white dome of the Shah Najaf and had been for two or three hours, I suppose.

To advance at Shah Najaf was our order − 93rd, 1st Madras Fusiliers, Peel with his sailors and one 24-pounder, and some Madras Sappers. Sir Colin led us himself for some way across the open, and we went over the plain and into a cluster of mud huts which lie almost under the outer walls of the place. Here Peel brought his guns within about thirty yards of the walls as if he were laying his frigate alongside an enemy's ship. The enemy kept up a withering fire on us, and our poor fellows were being knocked about dreadfully. The sun was setting; what with the 'sulphurous canopy' and the failing daylight, we couldn't see where we were, and it was crouching, undecided work, reminding me of the first advance on the Lahore Gate at Delhi.

An hour of this work had cost us no end of lives and all light had gone, but that from burning thatch, when it was decided that Peel's breach was no good (for the outer wall breached revealed only an inner one intact). The gun was withdrawn and the troops were being moved back, when, by luck, another breach was found, which had been made by the previous battering. In went the 93rd and the place was ours; into the garden went the glorious kilted boys and with the piper playing ahead made the circuit of the garden.

After this I went back and up to the European Barracks. It was night, and I didn't find our fellows, so slept in Remmington's Troop. We had only one alarm 'Stand to your Arms', and that was a false one.

17 November At daybreak I went to the European Barracks, where I found Stevenson and Pritchard with sappers, and three companies of 93rd. The barracks are in the form of a cross, and one mass of doors as barracks in this country generally are. The barrack itself we held, but the enclosure walls on the south and east were held by the enemy and from their loopholes they kept up a deadly fire on the building, through the multitude of open doors from which bullets came whistling at pleasure. We worked hard at closing all the openings with sandbags, shutters etc.

After some hours I was ordered off on another work: the Mess House (a great castellated building, supposed to resemble an ancient castle, with a stone moat and drawbridge) was to be taken. Forbes with twenty sappers was to throw a bridge over the moat (13 feet wide), and I with ten sappers was to lay mussocks [leather water-bags] of powder at the doors and blow them in — very pleasant work: had Pandy held out I don't see how Forbes, or I, or any of the sappers could have escaped unhit. We lay under shelter of some mud huts on the plain, and I arranged my mussocks, and powder hoses, and quick-matches, and gave directions to my men, and then we watched the reconnoitring. Forbes with some men went forward to see if our heavy pounding from big guns had dislodged the enemy or no. On they went, up to the circular mud wall of the garden: no opposition; into the garden: no fire from the enemy; so on more troops were sent, and in they went unopposed, and soon the British flag was flying on the roof. So my life is saved and my Victoria Cross gone, thinks I!

I was ordered to stay where I was, so lost the rest of the fighting. Our troops then carried the Moti Mahal, and presently cheers from house to house, gun to gun, regiment to regiment, down the road, conveyed the news that the junction was effected, and the Relief (as good as) effected. Outram, Havelock, Napier and Russell (Engineers) — the two latter wounded — had met Sir Colin. How we all did cheer! That night all the Gomati bank (right) was ours, from Residency to Dilkusha. After nightfall, I wandered back towards the European Barracks, but tired, and not easily finding my way, I bivouacked with the 23rd.

At nightfall, Keen with 70 of the 2nd Punjabi Infantry, passed silently, without whispering a word or firing a shot, through Pandy pickets, who crouched round their fires, to Banks's House in our left rear. Entering as the pickets there had just gone out to cook their food, they immediately barred them out and took possession.

18 November At daybreak I went to the Moti Mahal which was that day Engineer headquarters. Just outside it, the Naval guns were pounding away at the Kaisar Bagh. Pritchard and I were at work making a sort of sheltered way, a regular mockery of one, from Moti Mahal by Mr Martin's House to the Chattar Manzil.

During the day I went into the Residency and Palaces and saw the shattered buildings, the extraordinary barricades and batteries of mines, and all the wonders of that well-defended place. Some buildings only existed in memory, pounded into indistinguishable ruins. The great part of the besieged looked pale and ill, some very much aged and worn out. Walter was paler and thinner, but did not look ill.

Tobacco seemed to have been the principal want of the garrison; cheroots sold at 3 Rs. each! Dried guava leaves were considered treasures! As for drinkables, however, at the Relief there was a regular squandering of hoarded stores, and when Walter treated me to Moselle, it seemed hard to think of them as a starved garrison. They really were not in want of food, tho' spirits and tobacco, and vegetables were much wanted, and scurvy attacked many. The place, with its remains of what were once houses, its battered buildings, mines and batteries, was certainly a sight well worth seeing; this brave garrison have shown forth the invincible pluck of the British and will be remembered in history.

19 November During the night as we bivouacked in the Moti Mahal square, we had faint vision of people and doolies passing all night: these were the sick and wounded being carried away from the Residency. The Engineer officers were employed in making reconnaissances of the buildings we had captured. The Shah Najaf was my task.

20 November During the day, people and treasures and guns etc. were being removed from the Residency to Dilkusha. There was confusion all about Dilkusha, what with the Ladies, the sick and wounded.

21 November I was sent out in the morning to Dilkusha Park with some sappers to make an absurd demonstration of throwing a bridge of boats over the Gomati. The boats were perfectly useless and it is lucky that I had not really to make the bridge.

There was an attack on our position at Dilkusha, but doses of shot and grape from the guns sent Pandy off. The poor Ladies and the 'families' seem in great discomfort, tentless a great number.

23 November Yesterday I continued the 'demonstration' of making a bridge over the Gomati. Pandy attacked Dilkusha, but a few showers of grape etc. soon drove him off.

During the night all our people came out. Shaves say that a Highlander woke up in the European Barracks at ten a.m. and saw Pandies in platoons firing at a feather bonnet! He fled and escaped unseen!

We held across the river [canal] only Banks's House. I was ordered to make arrangements for taking Keen and his 100 men out. So my day was spent in making reconnaissance etc. I was told to raft them out: I decided on ladders up and down the broken arch of Dilkusha bridge to the debris in the channel, but I was shown a way across the dam of the Martinière bridge and along the opposite bank. I went that way to Banks's House. Keen greeted me, delighted to see at last a European in his lonely post. The roar of thousands in the city and the shouting and tom-tomming of the scoundrels under the very walls of the garden was very unpleasant to hear. The compound with its high walls and only one little hole of exit was a cul-de-sac, from which at sunset we glided out one by one like ghosts, crossed the dam and got back, happy to be free.

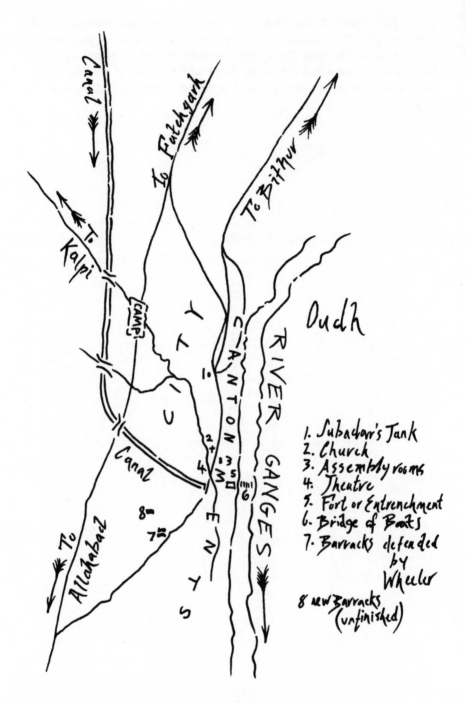

1. Subadar's Tank
2. Church
3. Assembly rooms
4. Theatre
5. Fort or Entrenchment
6. Bridge of Boats
7. Barracks defended
       by
     Wheeler
8 new Barracks
(unfinished)

CAWNPORE, DECEMBER 1857

144

CHAPTER 12

The Grand Army

Although Lang was personally responsible for bringing out the very last of the troops at the relief, his work on the bridge of boats had distracted him from observing earlier the tactics of one of those classic withdrawals for which ironically the British Army is especially famous. Sir Colin had brought the women, children, sick and survivors of the Residency safely out of the city under cover of what seemed to be a furious assault on the enemy strongpoint of the Kaisar Bagh. The enemy were convinced he was about to attack, and it was not until late on 23 November that they discovered that the Residency was empty and the whole relieving force too had withdrawn to Dilkusha.

However, despite the skill with which it was conducted, there was no doubt that the withdrawal gave the mutineers good reason to account it a victory for themselves. Sir Colin would only be able to justify his strategy if he returned speedily and carried out a genuine and successful assault on the Kaisar Bagh. This he intended to do, though his conception of speed was very different from that of impatient junior officers such as Lang. He determined first to gather an army big enough to ensure inevitable success.

Meanwhile he must make for Cawnpore. Sir Colin's decision to withdraw was largely based on his concern for the handful of troops he had left there, under General Windham. The enemy's Gwalior Contingent, under the command of their one good general, Tatya Topi, was known to be closing on Cawnpore. Sir Colin must now go to its rescue and destroy what was the enemy's major army.

24 November, Alam Bagh Grant's division and the Chief, with most of the sick families, marched for Alam Bagh. I was sent to the river to destroy the boats and bring away planking etc. I caught up the column on the march and learned to my surprise that poor General Havelock had died that morning. How uncertain is human glory! He was on a very short road to the highest honours.

I think we all felt the shame of marching away, as if beaten, from before Lucknow, but of course Sir Colin knows what he is doing. We encamped south of Alam Bagh, as before, but with Ladies and children interspersed, in extraordinary fashion, amongst us. One Lady got admission, as ill, in Stevenson's tent and completely turned him out, and at daybreak she got her mother and sisters also installed!

25 November, Alam Bagh General Outram's division marched in from Dilkusha and formed a second line behind us. They say that Pandy fired a Royal Salute in Lucknow! It is extraordinary to see how the Ladies are 'gypsying' it everywhere and anywhere about the camp.

27 November, Bani 26 November was a quiet day of halt which I spent in writing. Today we did not start till noon, and marching along slowly did not reach our camping ground, two miles beyond the Bani bridge, until sunset. Outram's division of about 2,500 men remained at Alam Bagh. Walter too stayed behind.

28 November, Near the River Ganges Started at 7 a.m.; marched all day, halting two or three hours *en route*. We halted within two miles of the Ganges. Heard (as yesterday) guns at Cawnpore all day. A few sowars appeared on our flanks. We did not get in till night and got rest about 12.

29 November, Banks of the River Ganges At night (oh was it bitterly cold) after about an hour's sleep, off I was sent to the river bank to throw up a battery. Soon after daylight we had five heavy Naval guns and three heavy R.A. guns playing away on the opposite bank of the river where Pandy was invisible among trees and bungalows. I was on duty among those guns all day on the bare, burning, glaring sands, while about half of our camp moved across the bridge of boats.

30 November, Outside Cawnpore At daybreak I crossed with difficulty the crowded bridge and joined our division encamped in the southern part of cantonments. We found Pandy in possession of the city and a great part of the cantonments: the Gwalior Brigade with their siege train, new troops, not yet taught our superiority and therefore plucky. They say that the Fatehgarh troops are also here, and that fiend the Nana.

On the 25th General Windham with about 2,500 troops moved out about seven miles and attacked these fellows, drove them back and took three guns. Then, fearing to be cut off from Cawnpore, he moved back some five miles; on which, of course, Pandy advanced. Out went Windham again and had to *retire*. It seems that our men misbehaved, got a panic and bolted, losing everything they had: camp, tents, property etc. Next day out went our fellows again, and were again licked! The 64th bolted, and lost 5 officers killed. So we found the Entrenchment and its new outwork defended by Windham, but Cawnpore in possession of Pandy.

1 December, Outside Cawnpore Now we are still being pounded by his guns: shrapnel bursting and roundshot bounding over our tents. (A shrapnel just hit my tent, and just now as I stood in Lennox's tent, another smashed into one of his boxes.) Sir Colin seems to have no dash, and we are all grumbling at his want of pluck. He would never have sent 4,000 men to storm Delhi and throw themselves into that immense city full of thousands of enemy, when with this fine army he is afraid to attack this comparatively small force and allows them to bully him. What we are going to do no one knows.

6 December, Cawnpore On the night of the 3rd, all the Ladies, sick and wounded, started for Allahabad. On the 4th, no advance, no news. Report says that a missing officer of the 64th was hung at the Massacre House gallows. On the 5th a reinforcement of 900 men joined us. That afternoon Pandy attacked our left, and our Horse Artillery fought him and drove him back; we stood to our arms for some hours but did not turn out. By this time of course we were most impatient to be let loose on Pandy and could see no possible reason why Pandy should be allowed to bravado us any longer; so were quite ready when at 7 a.m. we were ordered to strike tents and were marshalled in our respective places.

From the Fort, as furious a cannonade as possible was kept up so as to let it be supposed that we should attack in that quarter: the Church, Assembly rooms etc.. Meanwhile our Light Artillery and Cavalry were going off to the west, and Hope's and Inglis's brigades were also taking ground to the left, formed up near the new barracks in long lines. Greathed's brigade lay inactive about the south of the canal, guarding those outlets for escape.

I was in Hope's brigade and could see beautifully the steady advance of those lines, marching as if on a review parade, no noise and no hurry, but as sure and resistless as fate. Pandy hardly showed, but fired shot and shell, the round shot for the most part bounding over the long lines, and the shrapnel shells bursting overhead and showering bullets down. The casualties were very few, tho' of course occasionally a shot would pitch in, and on would go the line leaving one or two bodies on the plain. I fancy that all day our loss was only about twenty killed and wounded. Pandy could not stand this advance, the bonnets and kilts of the 93rd and 42nd looked too formidable, and he bolted.

We came on his camp (where we are now encamped) full of cattle, horses, tents, gharis, and rum (which was at once broached and spilt). Here the 93rd and 53rd were led away to the right, and took another camp of Pandy's at the Subadar's Tank. But the most of us, and Cavalry and Horse Artillery, pursued up the Kalpi road. All along the road we took gharis, cattle and guns. Before we returned, at sunset, Pandy retook a gun, and, with it and two more, opened on our troops here, on which the 38th charged and took the three guns. We took 16 guns (one 18-pounder, eight 9-pounders, two 24-pounder howitzers, three 8-inch mortars and two 5½-inch mortars). We returned here and bivouacked foodless and tentless.

7 December, Cawnpore We remained here not knowing what orders would come: we had no food or baggage and existed on parched gram [pulse] and mithais [sweetmeats] from Pandy's camp. At sunset our baggage came up and we encamped here. During the day the remainder of the enemy cleared out of Cawnpore.

8 December, Cawnpore We went into the city and about the whole place. An officer of 64th told me he had just seen the Ladies of six of his brother officers killed on the 28th, hardly to be recognised, as most of them had been mutilated. The city seems quite deserted by Pandy, and the shops are beginning to be reopened, though Salik Ram, the great bread contractor [merchant], was killed by two soldiers of the 53rd. I hope they will be most severely punished, as the man talks English perfectly, and it seems that he was killed only for the money he had about him.

A column went out in pursuit towards Bithur. I did not go. I had sprained my ankle and was unable to march. We hear that although they could not catch the long-legged Pandy they took fifteen guns. So now we suppose that all the Gwalior Contingent guns, excepting two 18-pounders at Kalpi, have fallen into our hands.

Our loss has been very slight, but I don't think we are half satisfied: after a long delay and Pandy having kept us at bay for so long a time, being allowed to insult us with impunity, it is very unsatisfactory to see that he has escaped us with no good corporal punishment.

13 December, Cawnpore The 4th Company of Royal Engineers has joined us, and Major Nicholson commanding it (a young fellow only regimentally a 2nd Captain) is Chief Engineer; he brings four subalterns to strengthen our roster. Major Nicholson has evidently always done regimental duty and is more like a strict little adjutant than an Engineer officer, fond of smart drills, pipeclay, *et hoc genus omne*. I fancy the 'Delhi' style of the Bengal and Punjab Sappers 'perplexes' him, our scorn of appearances and drill, our absolute sway over our men. I expect he will soon ask me to doff my peacock feather plume from my helmet! Perhaps, too, he may ask me to doff also my loose khaki tunic and jackboots, and my black pouches and belt etc., and request me to wear red and russia leather, and gold lace, and other pomps − a more glittering, but not one half so soldierly looking, set of harness. However, I hope he will let us 'gang our ain gait' and rub pipeclay into the Royals.

It will be a happy day for me when we march up country. I have had a fear of being sent to Benares, or of being kept at Cawnpore, as Executive Engineer, to build barracks, both hateful *in prospectu*, especially the latter. However, I trust I may get safe away with Grant's division; if I do not, I must try and submit patiently, tho' it will be a good lesson in self denial.

15 December, Cawnpore Our division is, I believe, delayed for want of boots and shoes! So small a matter may influence important movements.

In *The Friend of India* our defeat of the Gwalior Contingent on the 6th is most absurdly lauded, made thoroughly to eclipse Delhi: we appear no end of heroes. Now we, the real actors on the scene, see this claptrap laid before the public, and through our knowledge of these deeds now passing into history learn to take history, and the tales of other wars and battles, at their true worth. By my writing to you sober sense and true accounts of what happens and what we think, you have a true idea, perhaps, of what is going on, but we cease to be heroes; the unvarnished tale of our doings looks mild beside the usual style of narration of past battles and wars. Yet I don't say that we are not fighting as hard a war, and distinguishing ourselves less than actors in those battles. Most of our new regiments are Crimean ones, and we hear that the 'Crimea was nothing to this: this *is* fighting, this *is* service.' To compare our campaign with others, read the newspapers and historical accounts; but to know the truth believe mine.

17 December, Cawnpore We are still in *statu quo*. All our moves are kept very secret. Yesterday we actually had a cricket match in camp. We only played one innings each, and the cricket, I must say, was very bad, but none of us had played since last January. I only got 4, bowled 2 and caught one wicket.

At Bithur they found Azimullah's correspondence − quantities of letters from his fair friends at home − some written by really well-educated, talented young ladies, most beautiful composition, praising their 'glorious Eastern Sun' and 'Indian Prince'. (This fiend, you know, was the Nana's chief adviser, could talk English beautifully, and had been to England.) Such wonderful letters; if I wasn't writing against time I would give you some amusing extracts.

20 December, Akbarpur Here I am again on the march, again 'knocking about' the country. No more halting idly at Cawnpore, but tramping along the road, with the rumble of guns and the playing of bands, and no end of dust, of pitching and unpitching of tents, and wondering where the enemy is, and how many guns he has here or there, and seeing the country − all that makes up active campaigning. I still say 'a soldier's life is the life for me', and I am very jolly.

I sent off a letter to you on the 17th via Calcutta (of course, no road up country), and that evening, still lazy and stiff after cricket, I got orders to be ready at 9 a.m. next morning to join Brigadier Walpole's column, a column dispatched into the Doab, to restore confidence and our rule, punish and hang and settle and do whatever our Brigadier has orders to do.

I will introduce you to our little column. First on the march you will meet the fine blue-coated Afghan and Sikh troopers of the 1st Punjab Cavalry; next you will mark the sheen of the lances of three squadrons (not 300 men tho') of the gallant H.M.'s 9th Light Dragoons. Then will come rumbling along the five guns of Blunt's Troop of Horse Artillery, followed by the six heavier ones of Bourchier's Light Field Battery. Then you will be very pleased to observe two intelligent-looking officers of Engineers (Scratchley R.E. and Lang B.E.) followed by 25 Royal and 25 Bengal Sappers. Then you will hear the bugling (French fashion) of the dark column of the 2nd Battalion of the Rifle Brigade (my ink gets blacker as I think of them!). Then see the red tunics and red facings of that smart corps the 38th − and again a dark column, the 3rd Battalion of the Rifle Brigade. As to going further down the line and getting into the dust and jumble of the carts, elephants and camels of the baggage, why, I don't see any use in it, do you?

That column, which with fancy's eye you have just looked at, is quite good enough to polish off any enemy it will meet, and is game to go to Agra or Mainpuri or wherever it may be ordered. We are halting here today. Akbarpur seems to have been a very fine place and has two very grand tanks with buildings about them. In one of these we bathed last night, such deep cold water! Service for the men today at morning parade, service for the officers at 3 p.m. Of course, all the villages around here have been unsettled for the last six months, and the Nana's agents have been collecting the revenue in kind and in coin for him; some of the grain collected for Nana may now be sent into Cawnpore.

Scratchley, my Royal comrade, lives with me in my tent, and we both are honorary members of Blunt's Troop mess, so we get on very comfortably. The three Infantry regiments are, I expect, all very good regiments, but they are all griffs, just out and so uncomfortable, unused to Indian ways of marching.

27 December, Ajitmal Here we are spending the rainy season of Xmas in marching about, hanging and shooting, and not remembering 'charity' and 'good will to all men': not a very correct Xmas time. However, considering our ostensible employment we get on very jollily and don't think much about the enemy.

What a difference between your Xmas and mine! How pleasant to recall the cheerful fires in shining grates, the 'cosy' look of an English room in winter, the happy circle of dearly loved home faces, yours dear Mother smiling at your 'quiverful' of loving children. How I wish some jinn would answer when I rub my ring and carry me to have a look at you all now: or would change the scene which meets my gaze as I look out of the tent: the green gram and dull khets amongst which our tents are pitched, the mango groves and deep blue sky overhead, and give me instead the white snow-clad fields, the dark leafless trees and hedgerows, black ice-bound ponds, and houses sparkling at every window with the light of blazing fires in warm rooms; and transform Scratchley (a fine good fellow no doubt, who lies on a charpoy reading a novel) with a tribe of Langs from the Pa and Ma down to the smallest of Ellies (unknown infant but compared in imagination to a little jolly sister who sits on one's lap and rumples exquisitely starched collars and pricks one in the eye with a carelessly wielded scissor). My bearer (with his mouth full of chapatti) would be with advantage changed into some Betty or Edie or George Long of home associations.

But no jinn comes, and I think it more likely that I shall be off in an hour with Cracklow of the Horse Artillery to stalk after antelope among the Jumna ravines, than that I shall ask my bearer to bore holes in the heels of my boots previous to my walking over the snow with George, Robby etc. to Mr Harris's pond for a little skating. So I leave off dreaming about merry old England and chain down my imagination to this Indian reality and make my pen tell methodically the doings of

Brigadier Walpole, his column and more particularly those of Lt A. M. Lang.

On the 20th, 21st and 22nd we were at Akbarpur. Each day parties were sent out to different villages and sepoys were caught: if resisting, shot down; if not, hung, either in their own villages or brought to camp to meet their fate. Some good bags of game were made in the neighbourhood by officers going out.

On the 23rd we marched across country to Derapur. We adopted then (and since) an advanced guard to which the Engineers and Sappers are attached; so I can walk away at the head of the column free from dust and see the day break over the country, and either stalk or gallop, pistol in hand, after game if I see any. We marched through very pretty wild country on the banks of the Sengar. We had to ford the river, and the sappers had to make a road up the steep banks. The river is very pretty, full of water, and though very winding it runs fast and clear and has high banks and cliffs. We bathed in a very deep fast part that evening, despite fears of muggers.

Next day, the 24th, we marched to Sikandra. We were out shooting most of the day, and prowling round the town the rest of it. The Troops and Battery messed together and had a very jolly evening. On Xmas day, after service and breakfast, Cracklow and I went out on foot to the Jumna. The ravines along the river banks and for a mile inland are very pretty, and clothed with dwarf jungle. We winded down the narrow paths leading directly to the river, occasionally between high cliffs catching glimpses of the blue sheet of water. Shooting at ducks and alligators on the river bank, we wandered about until we saw armed natives collecting on the cliff above, lower down the river; on which we made off up the ravine paths again as fast as we could, not to be cut off from the open country where we could ride. On the 26th, we marched to Auraiya. There was a daur of course, and some men shot and some hung. This morning we marched 13 miles into Ajitmal.

30 December, Etawah Yesterday, the bugles woke us soon after one, and by the light of the moon we marched as hard as we could so as to surprise the enemy here at sunrise, while cold still rendered them stupid, and their heads and ears were still wrapped in blankets. However, we might have spared ourselves the trouble, for our enemy, more discreet than brave, bolted from here yesterday for their chief's headquarters at Fatehgarh. Some dozen of the enemy, too late in starting, took refuge in the tahsil, and to turn them out two companies of Rifles, a gun and some sowars were sent. For about three hours they kept us at bay, in a little house and courtyard, and we tried rushing in, which ended each time in some of our men being wounded. We threw live shells over as grenades; we gave them doses of blazing thatch; then at last Bourchier and Scratchley made a mine on the roof and brought it down on them. We extracted some poor women and children badly wounded, as their men had cut them with their tulwars.

31 December, Etawah This morning, as we were waiting for breakfast, up came some natives with two wild donkeys − precious donkeys − their saddle pads, ordinary looking affairs, stuffed with bundles of letters instead of hay. I got no end among them, articles the very look of which I was beginning to forget.

Give my best thanks for all. These are sadly anxious times for all in India, and I wish anything I could do could save your anxiety on my account. The gracious God who has preserved Dacres and Walter and me so wonderfully through such great dangers will I trust preserve us still. We are very jolly notwithstanding all the anxiety we give you at home: it is odd how soon one gets used to the danger of fighting: one marches out to a fight, or expecting a fight, with no more care than if it were a meet with the hounds, and if you could only be sure that we were all right we should enjoy it much more.

Wretched old 1857 died out quietly with us. Such a sad year I hope we shall never see again; to me individually it has been, in a point, a happy one, yet I don't fancy I shall recall it as a happy year. 1858 will bring happiness and peace to us all.

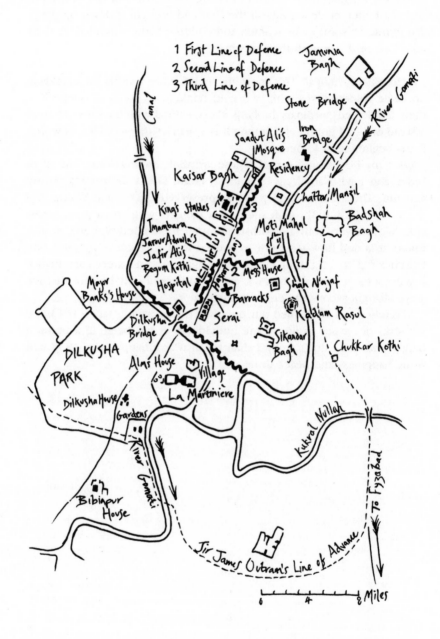

1 First Line of Defense
2 Second Line of Defense
3 Third Line of Defense

Jamunia Bagh

Canal

Stone Bridge

River Gomati

Saadut Ali's Mosque

Iron Bridge

Kaisar Bagh

Residency

King's Stables

Chattar Manzil

Imambara
Jarvur Adowla's
Jafir Ali's
Begum Kothi
Hospital

Moti Mahal

Badshah Bagh

Major Banks's House

Mess House

Shah Najaf

Dilkusha Bridge

Barracks

Serai

Kadam Rasul

DILKUSHA PARK

Alms House

Village

Sikandar Bagh

Chukkar Kothi

Dilkusha House

La Martiniere

Gardens

River Gomati

Kukral Nullah

To Fyzabad

Bibiapur House

Sir James Outram's Line of Advance

0   4   8 Miles

THE CAPTURE OF LUCKNOW, MARCH 1858

154

CHAPTER 13

The Last Battle

From Etawah, Walpole's column moved on to Fatehgarh where Sir Colin Campbell was with deliberate care concentrating his forces ready for the recapture of Lucknow. For the young Delhi veterans this was a frustrating time. They had taken Delhi against far greater odds. Why could not Sir Colin show the same dash? Why wait for even more of the troops making their way up from Calcutta?

Although Lang had by now made good friends of some of the Royal Engineers, and especially of Captain Nicholson, he was still sceptical of the calibre of those fresh out from England. How different were his recent companions in arms, many of whom he found waiting at Fatehgarh? 'They seemed still the same, still the plucky uncorrupted Delhi feeling, not yet spoilt by contact with English troops and Royal officers. How very, very superior are Indian officers and troops to the men and officers fresh from home!'

For Lang there was further cause for frustration. While the Grand Army rested 'in inglorious ease', he was appointed Executive Engineer at Fatehgarh, with responsibility for building barracks, and was due to be left behind when the army eventually left to attack Lucknow. Luckily at the last moment, in response to his repeated protests, a civilian engineer was sent to relieve him, and he was able to join the last column to leave Fatehgarh.

What he found at Cawnpore delighted him. Sir Colin had recognised the value of the Indian army veterans. Grant had a division, Wilson commanded the artillery, and, especially important for Lang, Robert Napier was to be Chief Engineer with Alex Taylor in charge of the Bengal Engineers. Also, to his delight, in addition to Walter Freeling and Dacres Wise, his great friend Elliot Brownlow was there too. They would all be together at the last great battle.

13 February, Camp Bani Here I am once more in Oudh, once more within sound of Pandy's guns, and again going to the 'front', to a good, famous battlefield I hope.

Yesterday I walked every step of the way from Cawnpore — twenty-two miles, and today marched ten miles to this place. Just before reaching Bani Bridge, we saw some fellows riding with greyhounds off on our right, so jumped in the saddle and rode up and found Fred Roberts and Watson out coursing and shooting. Nicholson, Maunsell and I joined them for a time. We saw a few quail and a teal brought down, and then went into camp.

The jolly pipes are skirling away as I write. Ahead we hear the booming of guns at Alam Bagh, where Outram's division is in a strongly fortified position. It is glorious being again amongst the 'pomp and circumstance of war'. Don't you envy me! Such a glorious big army too is drawing in on Lucknow, such smashing Artillery. Such a lot of Engineers and such a park, and as to the Infantry and Cavalry wouldn't I like to see them manoeuvred against Pandy on any of the big plains ahead!

15 February, Jalalabad Yesterday morning I walked with Taylor and Elliot Brownlow from Bani to Alam Bagh. We found the Engineers encamped on the right near Jalalabad. I found myself again amongst the jolly old set of Engineer officers. Immediately after breakfast Elliot and I walked over to Outram's headquarters and found Walter who was delighted to see us and came out to show us the front. We went to the left front village, where we have a picket and some light guns. There is a look-out and a telescope in that village and we had a good view of the Pandies in great numbers just out of rifle range, working away at rifle pits, batteries and trenches: coolies working, and red-coated, yellow-chevroned, havildars hectoring about, directing the works and occasionally throwing away bullets from rifle and musket. There are twenty-seven regular and thirteen irregular regiments of Infantry in Lucknow.

We went into Alam Bagh. The latter is no longer the choked depot of an army, only a strong advanced post held by 200 men. Only Outram's division is here — which originally we left here. The rest of the Grand Army covers the road between this and Cawnpore.

You may picture me to yourself as in my tent in the Engineer brigade

ELLIOT BROWNLOW (1832-1858)

Like Lang, his closest friend, Brownlow was the son of a EIC judge, did
well at Addiscombe and was posted to the Engineers (So was his elder
brother, Henry, who served with Lang at Delhi.). At Mian Mir, Lang had
introduced him to John Lawrence. 'Sir J. drew Elliot out on Kashmir,
pretending to know nothing. E. seemed nothing loth and rattled away as
if he did not feel the drawing. However the shrewd John must have seen
that his informant was an energetic, clever and very observant traveller.'
Lang knew he was, and for him Brownlow's death was the ultimate tragedy.
After that there was no more adventure.

camp, on the right of Outram's camp, near the old crumbling fort of Jalalabad. In my tent you may observe tables and chairs but no beds; for Elliot Brownlow and I share tents, his being our bedroom and mine our sitting room. A storm howls outside. It shrieks round our shaking and straining tents, and covers everything and everybody with a khaki gritty suit of dust.

I hope my next letter will tell you we have fairly opened the ball, and the next — a fortnight hence — that Lucknow is thoroughly ours and 'an awful sight' of Pandies have perished. After that happy event, I hope to get away and return to peace and quiet. Up at Lahore they seem at the Antipodes, having picnics and balls, and going on as peacefully and jollily as possible.

21 February, Jalalabad It's nearly a week since I sent off my last letter to you, yet I have little to tell you. Since the Engineer brigade came to Alam Bagh, no addition has reached Outram's division, and there has been as much monotony as if some uneventful work in peaceful times were passing in a slow cantonment.

Sir Colin dawdled a month at Fatehgarh, then like a flash of lightning, at a few hours' notice, went off for Cawnpore, leaving Fatehgarh weakly garrisoned. He went off thus, as all thought, to strike one of his rapid sudden blows, and has dawdled a fortnight since at Cawnpore. Since Sir Colin came out, Havelock or Neill or Nicholson (or even Greathed or Grant, blundering gallantly in their happy-go-lucky style) would have done fifty times as well. Any of those generals would have had their troops in summer quarters by this time, and all India ours.

My employment has been with Pemberton to superintend the making up of siege materials in the old fort of Jalalabad; so much of my day is spent there. In the evening we have great fun on the gymnastic bars, and strengthen our thews and sinews until time for dressing for mess.

Last night Pandy came out in very great force, and it was not till past noon that he was finally driven back. A large force of five regiments of cavalry with light guns nearly surprised the rear of camp, and some companies of sappers sent rapidly to form rear pickets held them at bay, till some of our light guns, the Volunteer Cavalry and 1st Sikh Cavalry came up and drove them to a safer distance, where they remained galloping about in squadrons over the open plain unable to muster pluck for a good charge.

Masses of infantry with scaling ladders came on against Jalalabad, but they could not stand the penetration of our bullets, which would kill two men, one behind the other. Those 'Minies' and 'Lancasters' do give us a wonderful advantage over Pandy, and he finds it very disagreeable to find the conical bullets dropping in at 1500 yards into his columns. He can hardly ever get the pluck up to venture within range of his own muskets. He must now mourn his folly in rejecting these same cartridges, which play such mischief with him.

2 March, Jalalabad My work remains the same, which chiefly means the preparation of brushwood and the manufacture of the same into gabions [cylindrical wicker baskets filled with earth], fascines, baskets etc. This work goes on from 5½ a.m. to 3 p.m. Thus you see that, tho' not hardly worked, I am rather bound to the camp till the evening. Gymnastics is the *play* of the day. On the 24th we Engineers had a very good match at football, but as several men were bruised and otherwise disabled, Taylor has never let us play again.

As we were at Jalalabad this morning, we saw Sir Colin, Outram, Lugard, Mansfield and other swells appear, and the advance guard of his force *en route* to the Dilkusha, march round the corner of the fort. He has with him the 2nd Division (Lugard's), the 1st Cavalry Brigade (Little's) with Artillery and Naval Guns. The 3rd Division is still at Banthra, and will come on, I suppose, tomorrow.

To see how has fared the day, Elliot, Greathed and I are going to ride over the four or five miles to Dilkusha, despite chances of Pandy sowars hovering about the fields.

4 March, Dilkusha To proceed with the tale where it left off: we three cavaliers pricked it o'er the plain without adventure, and on sighting the park wall of Dilkusha we came on some doolies of wounded and Brigadier Little shot through the elbow. Our troops held Dilkusha House and all the high ground of the Park. Pandy held the Martinière and Banks's House, and all between and beyond. His skirmishers were on our side of the canal and, as I foolishly galloped up on the brow of the hill, such a volley of bullets came pinging round the ears of this supposed general that I jumped off my horse *instanter*, and taking shelter behind a high wall spied our position. The avenues of trees between Banks's House and the Martinière were crowded with the enemy, and they were evidently bringing more guns up to oppose us. Peel was to the front ordering up his 24-pounders as usual to the open. No camp was pitched.

We galloped back to our own camp and found orders for marching at night. Walter and Dacres (now temporarily commanding Hodson's Horse) dined in our mess, and so we three at last sat down to one table.

I was up at 11 and rode off on the Banthra road to the rear serai picket to escort up the siege-train. It was a beautiful moonlit night and I lay down on a high mosque chabutra, from which I had a good view over the flat open plain, the only sound being the chirruping and humming of insects. At last, at about 2 a.m., I saw a black line winding on the plain. Clinking and clanking came a squadron of 7th Hussars, followed by the 23rd, and then by great Naval guns − the 68 and 24-pounders.

I led them along to Jalalabad, and spent till daybreak in forcing a clear way through all the outlets and inlets of Jalalabad, which were choked up with Engineer park carts, baggage etc. As day broke I had got a few guns through Jalalabad and on we marched, slowly overtaking the 1st Fusiliers, Engineers and Sappers, Hodson's Horse etc. We breakfasted under a tree on the road. We encamped behind Dilkusha Park, near the river in the grounds of Bibiapur House, a capital ground, retired, shady, abounding in lungoors [great white-bearded apes]. Bibiapur House is half-a-mile in rear of Dilkusha House. It is a fine double-storied house. We seized it as a mess house, but after breakfast this morning Sir Colin occupied it, and his HQ camp was pitched all round it. Our camp stretches from the Gomati on its right, across the Park (behind Dilkusha House) and the open ground outside. We expect Franks's column in today by the Sultanpur Road, and the 3rd Division, and more Cavalry and guns from Banthra.

6 March, Dilkusha After mess on the evening of the 4th, I was ordered out to select a route, and make a road if necessary, from Franks's camp on the Sultanpur Road to the point where we were to bridge the Gomati, and parties were sent down to the river bank to construct a bridge of casks. As it was pitch dark, and I had not the faintest idea of where Franks was, I did not admire my task. However, being an Engineer officer *of course* I found the camp. At daybreak I twice went over the ground and selected a direct route over the fields, and with sappers worked it up into a road.

Innes of our corps, who was with Franks, got the VC at Sultanpur, during an action where Franks took twenty guns. Innes found himself with a body of troops opposite three of Pandy's guns. Pandy deserted one, but the gunners stood to on nos 2 and 3, which bore on no 1. Our troops took no 1, but would not advance. Innes dashed up and shot a gunner of no 2 just as he was going to fire his gun. Then Innes, revolver in hand, rode up and down nos 2 and 3 keeping off the gunners, and tho' unsupported by our troops, who would not come on, and fired at by no end of Pandies from the buildings, for *seven* minutes he kept those guns, till Franks himself led on the men to his support. The men had been hanging back, saying: 'Look at that mad fool, Giglamps,' while the 'mad fool' was keeping off the fire of Pandies' grape from them. Then again on the 4th, while heaping up cartridges before a serai gate − the men would not help — he and a 97th officer kept running backwards and forwards themselves to do it, and both were wounded, the 97th officer mortally. Innes, with flesh wounds, is all right in our camp.

Last night Franks moved up, and today the 3rd Division crossed the Gomati under General Outram.

The spies say that a great number of the enemy have left Lucknow to hold and fortify a place somewhere in the jungle outside: a place to fall back on after they have been turned out of Lucknow itself, and that Pandy has fortified Lucknow strongly. You have my sketch of our last advance: look at it. [Lang is referring to map on page 134. He drew the map on page 154 after Lucknow was captured.]

I must have marked the sandy dry canal. Where it makes a sharp bend have I marked 'cliffs' on Pandy's side? Instead of entering the Gomati by that sharp bend to the right near the Martinière, imagine the canal continued straight to the Gomati. Along that straight cut we hear that Pandy has a line of works, with a ditch thirty feet wide before it. That is line no 1.

For line no 2 imagine a line whose left is Moti Mahal, centre Mess House, right Imambara. No 3 closes in the Kaisar Bagh, which is their citadel. So Pandy ought to make a very good stand indeed, and I hope we may manage to cut up a great number of them.

8 March, Dilkusha When Outram crossed the river on the 6th he cut up some thirty Pandies. He's pitched his camp on the Fyzabad road near a big bridge over the Kukral Nullah. (I will send you a plan showing the northern shore of the Gomati. [See map on page 154.]) I believe that tomorrow he will carry the Chukkar Kothi (the racecourse grandstand) and we will carry the Martinière.

10 March, Dilkusha Early yesterday morning General Outram carried the Chukkar Kothi easily, and pushed on, clearing the enclosures. By 10 o'clock he had possession of the Badshah Bagh, thus taking the first Pandy line of entrenchments in reverse.

At 1½ o'clock General Lugard advanced on the Martinière from the Dilkusha, the 42nd on the left, the 93rd and 4th Punjab Infantry on the right, supported by Bishop's Troop, with 200 Punjab Sappers attached. I was in command of the last, and had Thackeray and Forbes under me. Down the hill we came. Behind us (on the high ground before Dilkusha House) our heavy guns thundered on the Martinière. The 42nd were first let loose, and rushed at the huts about the Martinière Alms House. I was with the 93rd, who were very indignant, jealous and impatient, and when the right was let loose away we went at the double across the open in front of the building. Stumbling among the maze of trenches which Pandy had thrown up, we occupied the house and garden.

Pandy *of course* did not wait for us, but beat a judicious retreat, first to the ruined village between the Martinière and the canal, out of which he was driven in less than no time, and then to his high earthen ramparts across the canal. Our skirmishers pursued him nearly to the canal, and got good cover there. However, to our surprise and vexation they were recalled. I was set to work to loophole the Martinière garden, and fortify the village beyond. However, all came right in the end. From the village we saw some of the 42nd crossing from the Martinière towards Pandy's left bastion on the Gomati. We looked with telescopes. As Forbes and I were standing on a wall, and I was resting a telescope on his shoulder, 'thud' came a bullet and sent him spinning off the wall. Luckily he was only slightly wounded on the inside of the arm.

At last we see bonnets and crimson hackles on the ramparts, and white turbans running before them, tumbling helter-skelter from the bastion. Our Highlanders in the village laugh and shout and cheer and send Minie bullets pinging at the flying Pandies. The enemy's bastions on our left get vicious and send grape flying into the village. At last the 42nd get nearly opposite us, and our men are allowed to go on straight at the place. So by sunset we hold Pandy's canal line from the Gomati to within thirty yards of the Martinière bridge.

Very fine ramparts they are: the canal is the ditch from which rises a height of steep earth some thirty feet high, and here and there round bastions. I was at work till past midnight, cutting through this rampart and throwing a causeway across the canal, so as to make a nice road for the guns. I expect our casualties were very few: I had Forbes and five men wounded in my lot.

12 March, Martinière Observe our camp is moved. On the 10th we pushed on up the canal line of works to Dilkusha bridge and occupied Banks's House. The Sikandar Bagh was occupied by a picket in the evening: it was undefended.

Yesterday Outram forced his way through the suburbs and occupied the Iron and Stone bridges. He lost a good many. That fiend Pandy is taking it out of us in officers, and our men are very savage. They smoked and burned the men (I am afraid women too) who lay hid in huts near the Iron bridge and kept shooting our stragglers.

On this side we also advanced. On the right, Medley, Carnegie and I, being with 100 sappers at the Sikandar Bagh, and having a strong objection to the dreadful odour of the 1,840 Pandies half-buried there, and being pretty sure that the Kadam Rasul was deserted, took three sappers and stole into it and found it empty. From the top of it we saw the Shah Najaf seemingly also deserted. While Medley galloped to get General Lugard's permission to occupy it, I rode across the bridge of boats (which is now hauled up to just within the canal line of works) and warned the Artillery and Rifle posts across the river not to fire on us. (Our riflemen had fired on us when we went into the Kadam Rasul.)

So we moved into the Shah Najaf and fortified it. Pandy had done most of this for us. One of Outram's rear batteries kept up very nice practice *just* over our heads into the Mess House and Moti Mahal, and, at last, a little powder being short, in came a huge 8″ shell and cut off the arm of a 53rd man, as if a razor had done it!

On the left they advanced an hour before sunset, occupied the two furthest D bungalows, and carried the Hazrat Ganj Serai and Begum Kothi. At the latter they got a bag of 500 Pandies. The 93rd lost two officers killed, and were very savage, dragging out the bodies heaping them up, and making assurance doubly sure with the bayonet. To our grief, Taylor was shot through the thigh, so during this siege the best officer in the whole army will be *hors de combat*. We are also very much afraid that Hodson is mortally wounded.

13 March, Martinière I have returned from a long night's duty in the front, having gone down yesterday at 5 pm to the Begum Kothi. Poor Hodson died at 1 pm yesterday. I saw his body lying in Banks's in the evening. The finest Cavalry and 'Intelligence' officer in the army, he had no right to be at the Begum Kothi. He was shot by a scoundrel lying in a tykhana [underground room]; our fellows had made a hole into the roof of the tykhana, and as Hodson passed by he was shot. The 22nd have been pretty well exterminated, I expect: they seem to have been a very fine regiment, *Hindu sepoys*, and many of them died hard.

Last night it was beautiful to watch our shells rushing hissing into the air like so many fiery comets and falling one after the other in curves in the Kaisar Bagh and Mess House, then bursting to send flashes of light into the dark night and roaring reverberations among the courts of the native buildings. We had mortar batteries in the main street (Hazrat Ganj), and Outram had batteries far away on our right front across the river. One shot pitching into the Mess apparently blew up a big mine (probably meant for our benefit when we should storm that building) and sent columns of dust up and shook even the buildings amongst which we were. There arose shouts from the Pandies and the long monotonous sing-song of hundreds of women, as if they were mourning some great swell or numbers of heroes.

At daybreak we pushed on thro' a hole we had made at night and occupied courtyard after courtyard of the palaces known as Jafir Ali's and Jarour Adowla's until only a street separated us from the Imambara. There was no active opposition, and our men's bayonets were used against geese and fowls instead of Pandies.

I saw three new regiments of Jang Bahadur's Gurkhas march up to the front. Two are in red and one in blue. One of the red regiments seemed a very swell one, of Guards probably, in red coats and blue 'Zouave' pantaloons, with rifles, and moving in 'threes'. The officers wore silver epaulettes and leopardskin crossbelts and waistbelts. There are 16,000 Gurkhas here now.

I can report that Walter and Dacres, are well. Walter is sleeping in my tent tonight, and has been dining with us. He has come up from Alam Bagh, and saw Dacres *en route*, sulky at being out of the fun, and very jealous of me, who he declares always manages to be where the work goes on, and has all the news to send home.

14 March, Lucknow At 4 am I marched from camp with Medley and 150 men with ladders, crowbars etc., and Brownlow marched with a party carrying powder-bags. We went to our most advanced post. Our mortars were shelling the Imambara, and a great 68-pounder was sending its 8-inch shot smashing thro' the walls of the outer and inner courts, and breaching the main building itself.

We laid down our ladders, powder etc., ready to advance. But there was long delay, and it was even determined to have another big gun up for another breach, and we commenced making a road for it. However, a few of Brasyer's Sikhs reconnoitring got through the breach and into the inner court and, finding it empty, cheered and called out for supports. On went the rest of the regiment, and our sappers and other troops behind. Brownlow blew open a door, Pandy cleared out before us, and in a few seconds the whole Imambara was ours.

Some of our men, pushing further on, went out of the front gate of Imambara, crossed the Hazrat Ganj, and entered Pandy's second line of works. How Pandy did run! They passed in hundreds and hundreds across the open from the buildings about the European Barracks towards the Mess House, exposed to our flank fire. Our men were so excited and flurried that they did hardly any execution. It was such fun to see some come running out of the houses across the street and jump back startled on seeing our men behind their line of fortifications.

Our troops pushed on, along the rear of the Imambara, and along the back of the King's Brother's house, pushing on and on with Pandy in a panic and in full retreat. Before we knew where we were, we were among the first courtyards of the Kaisar Bagh. Our troops filing into a thin line in a wonderful way rushed into houses and courtyards till the line was spun as fine as could be, and was broken too: knots of twenty or thirty men held isolated points, and it was a mercy Pandy did not take heart and fling large bodies of men on our leading parties; we must have been cut off. Our orders had been only to storm the Imambara, and it was never supposed that we were going to carry the Kaisar Bagh. Consequently, no supports were ready.

The news flew back to camp, and in time regiments came up and secured our conquests. But meanwhile our position was precarious. However, in the Kaisar Bagh we were, and in very many parts of it. At one time I was with Brasyer and twenty Sikhs in the new palace (the very farthest point we reached and which we had to give up). Such desecration it seemed our rushing in: soft carpets which silenced the footfall, rich silk hangings, mirrors and chandeliers, tables covered with articles of vertu and bijouterie fresh from Regent Street and La Rue de la Paix. Of course, the Sikhs were at once employed in smashing up everything for gold and silver.

I went to the roof and coming down found no one but four Sikhs. We forgot how we had entered and went out on the wrong side and wandered in courts out of which we could not find the way. Presently came a volley of bullets, with shouts of 'Maro Firinghi Soor' [Kill the foreign pigs], and I thought I should be caught, for I was in a cul-de-sac, knew no way out and, even if I was only wounded, I must be captured. We rushed desperately at every door attempting to smash it open, and tho' urged by desperation, fired at, bullets smashing on the walls about us, we could not get through; at last I sprang up at a Venetian window with all my force; it gave and I tumbled into a room and saw light beyond; the four Sikhs followed me through the building into another court, and through a gateway, and saw some of our men.

More troops were sent up, and we gradually began to clear each range of buildings, each palace and summer-house. While clearing a suite of rooms, we discovered some Pandies skulking about in a garden. We left a few men at the windows, and went beating carefully through the garden. One of our watchers came to say that they were killing one another, and so we found fourteen lying in a heap dying in one corner. Our men made all sure and carried off their horses and two small guns.

In camp they would not for some time believe that we had the Kaisar Bagh. Our carrying it all so fast was a glorious bit of pluck and luck. It was a splendid palace: magnificent and gorgeous, yet much more tasteful than most native buildings: such jolly gardens, with marble honeycombed arbours, marble canals and high bridges, and *such* loot — jewellery and shawls, gold and silks! I was *knee*-deep in valuables, and yet did not improve my chance. Seeing that I did not help myself, a man held up a bag full of jewels — a bag as big as his head — and said: 'Take a share, sir. Take this.' Like a fool I came the magnanimous and rejected everything! I took some handsome tulwars which I stuck in my belt. One officer in the tent next to mine has upwards of 500,000 rupees worth of diamonds, pearls and rubies! I never saw such precious stones as I have here.

15 March, Lucknow We did not advance. The day was spent in looting and securing our conquests: many more Pandies who had remained hidden were killed about the Kaisar Bagh; a good many mines pointed out by spies were exploded or destroyed. I rode down to the Kaisar Bagh in the evening and found all the splendid buildings completely gutted.

16 March, Lucknow Walter came to breakfast; he is in Franks's camp. After breakfast I rode down with Maunsell to the Kaisar Bagh and from the top of Saadut Ali's mosque I watched the Pandies returning by hundreds from across the river over the Stone bridge. They crossed to attack Outram or to bolt, and were headed by our column on the Sitapur road. Our troops were pushed on and captured a 9-pounder at the Iron bridge laid for Outram's troops. Elliot behaved most gallantly and pluckily all day and was especially remarked. I spent the day in surveying Pandy's three lines of works.

17 March, Lucknow Elliot did not return until late, about 3 am. After breakfast Napier issued out to join Outram in carrying the rest of the city. Hutchinson asked Elliot to accompany, which he did, and I too went, tho' I had been told off to survey. We advanced, after long delays, along the back of the Jamunia Bagh, and almost immediately there was a halt. A street was nearly choked with gharis full of dubbas [jars] of powder, apparently Pandy ammunition deserted in rapid flight. I was ordered to bring up men to remove and drench it. Passing I saw Capt Clerke and some of his Royal Engineer company, and I told him my errand; he moved up to commence work (Elliot was with him). I rode further to the rear and got some men at last, but, so choked were the streets, had difficulty, providentially for me, in getting them up to the front.

Before I got back, I heard the rumbling of powder and saw a black column rise up. I rushed on to see: there were charred and burning carts, burst dubbas, scorched bodies of men, some bodies inaccessible for the fire. With horror and despair I hunted fruitlessly for Clerke and

Elliot, longing yet dreading to find them. At last a man brought Elliot's sword and said that he had been carried away.

I followed the doolies, searched all, and at last heard my name. Poor fellow, Elliot was so scorched I should not have known him: his face was black and I thought he was blind, but he said he could see with one eye. He said he knew he should die, but was quite prepared and did not fear. He was, of course, in dreadful pain, and very nearly sank before the long road to the Kaisar Bagh was traversed. I walked by him, fed him with water all the way. When he got in they rubbed oil over him, and he was given a little brandy and water which revived him. Poor Clerke had been brought in before, speechless and unconscious, and he died in an hour or so. Elliot bore up nobly and entirely from *Christian* fortitude, and never complained, though in dreadful agony.

I was so glad to have been by his death-bed, as he said that he had always prayed that I might be at his death-bed and he was so thankful that his prayer had been answered. I don't think a man could have died in greater faith. For a long time he would take no opiatives, for fear of dying insensible, but at last we persuaded him to take laudanum. That had effect and quieted the pains and he gradually fell asleep and sank and died in his sleep. God grant that I may meet my end as hopefully as he did his. He died about midnight.

Taylor, wounded as he was, was brought down in his doolie from camp to see him. No officer was more loved and respected in our brigade. I miss him every hour. We were always together, and I keep even yet finding myself instinctively thinking of him, and each time I am shocked at remembering the truth that he is no longer here.

18 March, Lucknow At daybreak Greathed and I made all the arrangements for his funeral. Poor Clerke and twelve of his men were dead. At 1½ pm the funeral took place, nearly all our officers attending. Clerke and his men were buried in one grave, and dear Elliot near them. The graves are in a cypress garden of the Kaisar Bagh. Walter came to the funeral and I returned with him.

25 March, Lucknow Since the 19th I have been perpetually at plans. My three colleagues and I have turned out two grand plans, each about the size of a large table cloth, illustrative of the operations, one for the Governor-General, and one for the Commander-in-Chief to send home. This is very hard work, especially to me, as I am the responsible party.

Yesterday I took a plan over to Napier. Sir Colin came in and after a proper amount of humbug, telling me how 'our little Queen, a curious little lady,' would pore over it etc., told me to add a lot more and work it up more; so I worked again till sunset.

The death of my dear friend Elliot has of course cast a gloom over the campaign as far as it concerns me, and has rendered it distasteful to me, and spoiled all my pleasure in war and victory and Lucknow. He was a friend such as I can never find again in this world, more than a brother to me. He would have sacrificed himself in any way to have benefited me. He was such a splendid fellow, a man destined, anyone would have said, to win the highest renown and to carve a great name for himself; energetic beyond comparison, of wonderful physical powers, cheerful and amiable, and an exemplary Christian. In him the corps has lost its finest young officer, and I have lost such a friend as I can again never find. God bless him.

CHAPTER 14

Epilogue

The capture of Lucknow effectively marked the end of the Mutiny. It would be a year before all resistance was ended, but life for the British could now return to something close to what they considered normal. Men could marry, and women be given in marriage, houses be bought and professions resumed − or they could so long as there was nothing more immediate to be done. Most soldiers were, for instance, eager to play a part in destroying the last pockets of Pandy resistance, as that way lay further opportunity to enhance their reputations and gain promotion. They were in no hurry to get back to cantonment life. Yet with a determination that amazed and even disturbed his friends Arthur Lang, of all people, now set out to do exactly that.

One reason was that Sarah was desperately anxious that he should do so. She had worried for his safety long enough. Regardless of his career or of the needs of the British army, she wanted him back home. There was, however, a further, and probably still more powerful motive: Lang had fallen out of love with war.

He had been extraordinarily lucky throughout the months of fighting, right up to and during the final battle for Lucknow. Not only had he personally led an almost charmed life, but his nearest and dearest had been almost equally fortunate. All three of the cousins had come through unscathed. Of the Boileaus only Frank had been wounded and he was well on the way to recovery. Above all, in the last battle he and Elliot Brownlow had been able to fight side by side through one of the fiercest and most exciting actions of the whole campaign, and both had come out unscathed. Then, when it was virtually all over, Brownlow had been killed − in a pointless, accidental explosion.

For Brownlow's greatest friend the shock was appalling. Lang was brought face to face, almost for the first time, with what it meant to lose a loved one. He had often speculated in his journals on how terrible such losses must be, and had been inspired by a righteous thirst for vengeance on behalf of his friends — but now he had himself lost someone he loved, and knew how that felt. The effect on him was the reverse of what he had expected. He wanted no more vengeance. He had had enough of it, and enough of this war.

There was in Arthur Lang's mourning for his friend something of the Old Testament intensity of David's lament over Jonathan, which his own background made it almost impossible for him to express adequately. At this moment it was Brownlow not Lang who supplied the appropriate commentary — in a letter that tells us in some ways more about Lang than he ever dared to commit to paper himself.

Back in Mian Mir in April, 1857, just before going to Kashmir on a mission that he believed might lead to his death, Elliot Brownlow had written two letters that would not be read by anyone until March, 1858. One was to the aunt who had brought him up after his mother's death. The other was addressed to Arthur Lang. 'My dear Arthur,' it began. 'You will never see this unless I am dead. Don't regret me as I believe that if I die I shall go direct to a happier world. That you were under the Divine Providence the means of bringing me to abandon a course of folly and sick for true happiness at the throne of grace has been the cause of making me love you with an affection and respect I have never felt for any other man of my own age. May God Almighty bless and prosper you and enable you to keep steadfast in the course you have so well begun. If so we shall soon meet in Heaven.'

Neither in this, nor in the letter to his aunt, which urges her to lose no time in making Lang's acquaintance as 'he knows me better than any other man in the world', does he indicate how or when Lang altered his life so significantly. It was not the kind of thing gentlemen wrote about in their diaries or journals. We only know that it happened, and may assume that it was an essential part of their close friendship. Certainly it adds to the poignancy of that scene in the crowded streets of Lucknow, and helps us to understand at least something of the trauma Lang suffered that day, and why he later behaved in a way that seemed to his friends totally out of character.

First he demanded to be sent back to the Public Works

Department in Lahore, only to be told bluntly that Lahore was not in need of engineers. Oudh and the North-West Provinces, and of course the columns that were being sent out in pursuit of the Pandies, were all short of engineers. That is where someone of his reputation would be welcomed, and where the road to advancement was to be found. In fact the Chief Engineer, Robert Napier, who at Lucknow had established a reputation that would lead him rapidly to the position of commander-in-chief, gave Lang a golden opportunity to follow in his train. 'He offered me the Brigade Majorship, which I declined, to his anger I am afraid,' Lang recorded ruefully. 'He knows I want to go back to Lahore and be married, and will perhaps let me go, tho' of course he chaffs me on the absurdity of leaving the country where all the appointments and all the army are, to return to a comparatively dull empty field.'

It was ironic that a man who had done so much over the last year to get away from the duties of an executive engineer was now so set on getting back to the Public Works Department. It was equally ironic that when he eventually got his way, in May, 1858, he found himself not in his beloved Punjab, but still stuck in Lucknow, as Assistant to the Chief Engineer in Oudh. He seemed to have got the worst of all the options. He had missed his chance of consolidating his reputation as a fighting soldier, while still being cut off from Lahore and his fiancée.

Unperturbed, he immediately arranged to bring Sarah to Oudh. They were married on 1 September, set up their first house in Lucknow, just in time to greet his brother George on his way to his first post in the Indian Civil Service. By the end of the following year a third brother, the happy-go-lucky Monty, had also stayed at their house, as a cornet in the Indian Army. By then Arthur and Sarah Lang had had the first of their children, and had established the style of life they were to pursue, with only the occasional change of house, quite contentedly for the next thirty years.

The rest of his professional career was to be distinguished without being particularly glamorous, as most of it was spent constructing buildings and roads, rather than the railways and canals which attracted most attention. He was an extremely popular principal of the Engineering College at Roorkee for six years, before succeeding his old friend Alex Taylor as Deputy-Inspector General, Military Works, and Secretary of the Defence Committee. Then he was appointed in turn: Superintending Engineer, Beluchistan; Chief Engineer and Secretary for Public Works in Burma, and finally Chief Engineer and Joint Secretary for Public Works in the N.W. Provinces and Oudh.

Professionally his was a valuable, satisfying career, yet hardly what his contemporaries at Addiscombe and Delhi would have expected. Many of them went on to become generals, even field-marshals. They would have expected the same of the winner of the Pollock Medal and the hero of the Kashmere breach. Yet, was that what Lang ever really wanted for himself? He seems genuinely to have preferred the life of the PWD engineer. Just before the outbreak of the Mutiny his friends were urging him to apply for the command of the Pontoon Train. It would have brought promotion, more money, the chance to make a name for himself. The one disadvantage was that it was unclear where he might go on from there. He agonized over the opportunity, then turned it down. 'The PWD is our proper profession out here,' he wrote home, 'and it is well to accustom myself to it, and go steadily up the ladder.' He was not looking for glory, just the chance to practise his engineering skills.

Above all, as his obituary in *The Indiaman* was to conclude, Lang 'delighted in his home. His family affections and friendships were particularly tender, and if success in life be gauged by personal happiness it must be owned that he had been abundantly successful.'

Indeed it was for his gentleness and humour that he was eventually to be best remembered. His home became the focus of family gatherings of both Boileaus and Langs, and by his retirement in 1888, he and Sarah were to have eight children of their own.

By then too he was an authority in the entomological world, and had made a collection of Himalayan and other Indian butterflies and moths, among which were specimens previously unknown to science. This collection he left in the keeping of the Calcutta Museum, a symbol perhaps of a love for India that in the end survived and transcended the tragedies of 1857.

He and Sarah came back to England, and set up house in Blackheath, only for Sarah to die the very next year. In 1893 he married Edith Lang, the daughter of his first cousin, and had one further child, a daughter, in 1897. Edith died in 1904, and he married again, Ida Richardson, in 1905. He himself died in 1916.

The friendships he forged in India, and especially during the siege of Delhi, remained tremendously important to him, though he seldom talked of the Mutiny to those who had not been there. Occasionally the survivors met to reminisce on their own, and in

June, 1907, the fiftieth anniversary of the Mutiny, there was a commemorative dinner and a levee at Buckingham Palace. It was an opportunity for Lang's friends to raise with the Palace a matter that had been overlooked for fifty years – that alone among the Mutiny heroes Lang had had no public acknowledgment of his heroism.

In 1857 and 1858 he had been mentioned in despatches four times (twice at Delhi, once at Agra, and once at the Capture of Lucknow). He had also been recommended for the VC on three occasions (at Delhi, at the Relief, and the Capture of Lucknow). Yet he had not received the VC, nor had he been rewarded with high rank. Nowhere in the diaries or the journals are there any references to these recommendations or to being mentioned in despatches, nor is there any evidence that Lang himself either noticed the lack of public acknowledgment, nor that if he did he minded it. His friends, however, had. The history of his Corps expressed their feelings: 'Arthur Lang, who as all agreed had earned many Victoria Crosses but received none.'

On 25 June, 1908, the Palace did what they could to set matters right. Lang noted the news in his diary on that day, in characteristically laconic style. Meticulous as always, he noted the weather conditions, and then devoted eight lines to the mowing of the lawn, a game of croquet, and the book the family read aloud that evening. Then he added, unusually, a separate paragraph: 'Birthday Honours contain CB for Colonel Arthur Moffatt Lang, Royal (Bengal) Engineers (Retired).' That was all. That was enough.

Arthur Moffatt Lang at the age of 77

GLOSSARY

This glossary covers those words (mostly Indian) the meanings of which cannot be found in a single-volume English dictionary. Explanations of these words are also given in the text in square brackets, but only on their first appearance.

Abattis	A tree entanglement
Bara Dari	Reception hall
Baboos	Clerks
Babul	Acacia
Berm	The flat space of earth between the foot of a defensive wall and the top of the ditch below
Bhisti	Water carrier
Cantonments	Army barracks
Carcasses	Incendiary shells
Chabutra	Seating platform
Charpoy	'Four-footed' — a light Indian bedstead
Chota Hazri	Light breakfast
Contractor	Merchant
Cossid	Courier or messenger
Counterscarp	Side of a defensive ditch facing the defenders
Cutcha	Incomplete, rough
Cutcherry	Courthouse, office
Dak	Postal service. A Dak Bungalow was a barely furnished building where travellers could stay
Dauring	Raiding
Doab	The land between the Rivers Ganges and Jumna
Doolie	Covered litter or stretcher
Diwan-i-Khas	Hall of private audience in Imperial Palace
Durree	Counterpane
Dubbas	Large Jars
Ekkas	Light two-wheeled carts
Fascines	Long bundles of brushwood, tied tightly together
Firinghis	Derogatory term for Europeans
Gabions	Wicker baskets filled with earth
Ghat	Wharf
Glacis	An open level space on the attackers' side of a ditch open to the defenders' fire
Gram	Pulse
Ghari	Cart
Gharib parwar	An Indian compliment: 'Protector of the poor'
Ghazis	Moslem fanatics devoted to the killing of infidels
Grape (shot)	Bags of bullets etc, fired from guns
Grasscut	A servant who collects grass for horses
Griff	New arrival in India

Havildar	Indian Army Sergeant
Jhil	A swamp
Kanauts	Tent walls
Keranies -ses	Eurasians
Khets	Fields
Kunkur	Limestone
Khit	A servant who waits at table
Lakh	100,000 units, usually of Rupees
Lathi	Thick iron-bound stick
Lumbardar	The registered headman of a village
Maidan	An open plain
Mata Deens	A common name for the natives in Oudh, from which the mutinous sepoys very largely came
Mazbis	Sikh road sweepers
Mithais	Sweetmeats
Mussocks	Leather water-bags
Nuands	Earthenware pots
Omlah	Court clerk
Pachisi	A game played with counters, similar to Ludo
Palka-ghari	A covered cart
Pandy (ies)	Nickname of the mutinous sepoys — after Mangal Pande who defied the British at Barrackpore
Poorbyas	Punjabi term for sepoys from Oudh and Bengal
Puggree	Light turban
Pukka	Correct. Applied to a house, it signifies that it is built of burnt brick, not sun-dried brick
Ram Sammy House	English slang for a pagoda — a corruption of *Ramaswami* (Hindus)
Rezai	Counterpane
Risaldar	Indian cavalry officer
Seer	Approximately 2lbs in weight
Serai	An inn
Shave	A false alarm (English slang)
Shazada	Indian Prince
Syce	Groom
Sowar	Horseman — either cavalry or police
Tahsil, -dar	Revenue office, Revenue officer
Tank	Artificial lake
Tat	Pony
Tiffin	Luncheon, light meal
Tope	Grove of trees
Tulwar	Indian sword
Tumbril	Two-wheeled covered cart
Tykhana	Underground room
Wilayati	British
Zenana	Quarters for women in Mohammedan houses

The Family Tree of Arthur Moffatt Lang
(Asterisks identify those members of the family mentioned in the book)

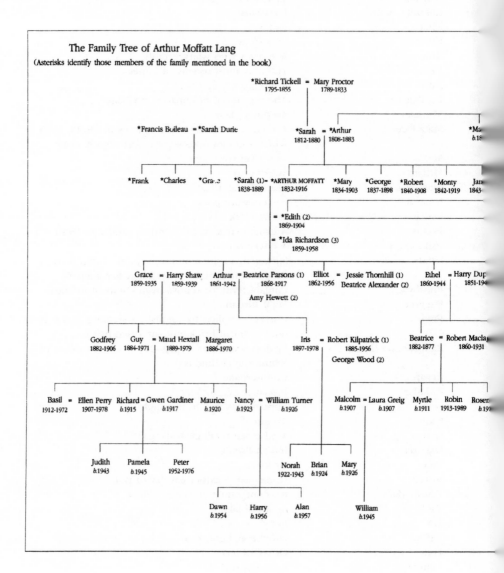

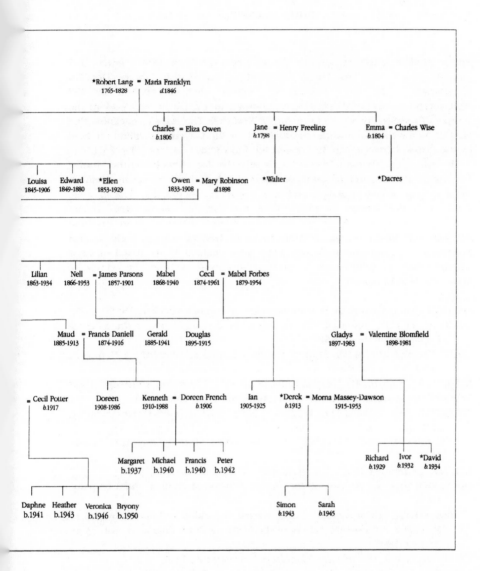

*Robert Lang = Maria Franklyn
1765-1828   d.1846

Charles = Eliza Owen   Jane = Henry Freeling   Emma = Charles Wise
b.1806   b.1798   b.1804

Louisa   Edward   *Ellen   Owen = Mary Robinson   *Walter   *Dacres
1845-1906 1849-1880 1853-1929   1833-1908   d.1898

Lilian   Nell   = James Parsons   Mabel   Cecil = Mabel Forbes
1863-1934 1866-1953 1857-1901   1868-1940 1874-1961 1879-1954

Maud = Francis Daniell   Gerald   Douglas   Gladys = Valentine Blomfield
1885-1913 1874-1916   1885-1941 1895-1915   1897-1983   1898-1981

= Cecil Potter   Doreen   Kenneth = Doreen French   Ian   *Derek = Morna Massey-Dawson
  b.1917   1908-1986 1910-1988   b.1906   1905-1925 b.1913   1915-1953

Margaret Michael Francis Peter   Richard Ivor   *David
b.1937   b.1940   b.1940   b.1942   b.1929   b.1932 b.1934

Daphne Heather Veronica Bryony   Simon   Sarah
b.1941 b.1943   b.1946   b.1950   b.1943   b.1945

BIBLIOGRAPHY

Arthur Moffatt Lang's manuscript diaries (from 1857 to 1859), letters and journals (from 1851 to 1862) are held in the British Library Dept of Manuscripts (Add. Mss. 438818 to 438825). Extracts, edited by Col Molesworth and Lt-Col Leslie, were published in 1931/2 in vols 9-11 of the *Journal of the Society for Army Historical Research.* The maps of Lucknow that Lang drew for the Commander-in-Chief and for the Governor-General are held by the British Library (Map 3c 17) and the India Office Library (Map F5 14).

The following bibliography is a highly selective list of books on the Mutiny. It is concentrated generally on those books that have been especially useful in the checking of historical fact, and includes several books that deal in some detail with the actions in which Lang was engaged. Those that contain references to Lang's adventures are marked with asterisks. Most of these accounts are based on the reminiscences of General Taylor, Field Marshal Roberts and Major-General Medley. Only those marked ** are based on their authors' study of Lang's own account, almost exclusively in the edition of Molesworth and Leslie.

*MEDLEY, Julius George, *A Year's Campaigning in India*, Thacker, 1858

MECHAM, Lt C.H., and COUPER, G., *Sketches and Incidents of the Siege of Lucknow*, London, 1858

*BALL, Charles, *The Indian Mutiny*, London Printing and Publishing Company, 1859

RUSSELL, Sir William, *My Diary in India*, Routledge, Warne and Routledge, 1860

*VIBART, H.M., *Heroes of Addiscombe*, Archibald Constable, 1894

*ROBERTS, Field Marshal Lord Frederick, *Forty Years in India*, Richard Bentley, 1897

*KAYE, John W., and MALLESON, H., *The Indian Mutiny*, Longman's Green, 1897

GOUGH, General Sir Hugh, *Old Memories*, William Blackwood, 1897

*RICE HOLMES, T., *History of the Indian Mutiny*, Macmillan and Company, 1898

*BAIRD SMITH, Lt-Col Richard, *Delhi Journal*, expanded and edited by Col H. M. Vibart, Professional Papers of the Corps of Royal Engineers Vol. 23 pp 87-130, 1897

TROTTER, Lionel, *Life of John Nicholson*, John Murray, 1898

VIBART, Colonel Edward, *The Sepoy Mutiny*, Smith Elder, 1898

*THACKERAY, Edward T., *Biographical Notices of Officers of the Royal (Bengal) Engineers*, Smith Elder, 1900

*FITCHETT, W.H., *The Tale of the Great Mutiny*, Smith Elder, 1902

YULE, H., & BURNELL A., *Hobson-Jobson: a glossary of colloquial Anglo-Indian words and phrases*, Routledge and Kegan Paul, 1908

MAUNSELL, General Sir F.R., *The Siege of Delhi*, from *Royal Engineers Journal* July, 1911, and *Nineteenth Century and After* October, 1911

*TAYLOR, Alicia Cameron, *Life of General Alex Taylor*, Williams and Norgate, 1913. These volumes include material that was apparently contributed directly to the author by Arthur Lang.

GILLIAT, Edward, *Heroes of the Indian Mutiny*, Seeley, Service, 1914

GILBERT, Henry, *The Story of the Indian Mutiny*, George Harrap, 1916

**SANDES, Lt-Col E.W.C, *The (Royal) Bengal Engineers*, Institute of Royal Engineers, Chatham, 1937

PEARSON, Hesketh, *Hero of Delhi*, Collins, 1939

**SANDES, Lt-Col E.W.C., *The Indian Sappers and Miners*, Institute of Royal Engineers, Chatham, 1948

WOODWARD, Philip, *The Men Who Ruled India; The Founders*, Cape, 1953

*LEASOR, James, *The Red Fort*, Werner Laurie, 1956

SEN, Surendra Nath, *1857*, Delhi, 1957

POLLOCK, John, *Way to Glory (The Life of Havelock of Lucknow)*, John Murray, 1957

HILTON, Major-General Richard, *The Indian Mutiny*, Hollis and Carter, 1957

MACLAGAN, Michael, *Clemency Canning*, Macmillan, 1962

**COLLIER, Richard, *The Sound of Fury*, Collins, 1963

EDWARDES, Michael, *Battles of the Indian Mutiny*, Batsford, 1963

HEWITT, James, *Eye-witnesses to the Indian Mutiny*, Osprey, 1972

**HARRIS, John, *The Indian Mutiny*, Hart Davis MacGibbon, 1973

EDWARDES, Michael, *A Season in Hell*, Hamish Hamilton, 1973

EDWARDES, Michael, *Red Year*, Hamish Hamilton, 1973

CHAMBERLAIN, M. E., *Britain and India*, David and Charles, 1974

MASON, Philip, *A Matter of Honour*, Jonathan Cape, 1974

BARR, Pat, *The Memsahibs*, Secker and Warburg, 1976

LLEWELLYN, Alexander, *The Siege of Delhi*, Macdonald and Jane's, 1977

ELLIOT, James, *India*, Batsford, 1977

**HIBBERT, Christopher, *The Great Mutiny India 1857*, Allen Lane, 1978

SONGHAL, D. P., *A History of the Indian People*, Methuen, 1983

**PERKINS, Roger, *The Kashmir Gate*, Picton, 1983

**MONTGOMERY, Brian, *Monty's Grandfather*, Blandford, 1984

ALLEN, Charles, *A Glimpse of the Burning Plain*, Michael Joseph, 1986

**BROEHL, Wayne G. Jnr, *Crisis of the Raj*, University Press of New England, 1986.

LAWRENCE, John, *Lawrence of Lucknow*, Hodder and Stoughton, 1990

INDEX

Italics refer to maps and illustrations. L = Arthur Moffatt Lang. All military formations are listed under REGIMENTS. Ranks are those held during the Mutiny. NI = Native Infantry; BE = Bengal Engineers. 'Siege' and 'Assault' refer to the siege and assault of Delhi; 'Relief' and 'Capture' to the second relief and capture of Lucknow. 'Column' refers to the columns from Delhi to Cawnpore and Lucknow, and from Cawnpore to Fatehgarh.

Benson, George, Bengal Civil Service: death at Relief 140
Best, Capt Henry, 1st Punjab Cavalry: in Column 103
Bewar: *110*; Column at 119
Bibiapur House and Village: *154*; at Relief 136; at Capture 160
Bijegarh: *98*; Column at 109
Bithur: *38, 110*; women and children killed 59; pursuit towards 148; Azimullah's letters at 150
Boileau, Lt Charles, 61st Hill's: at Siege 44, 57, 60, 71; with Foot Artillery 80, 83; rejoins 61st 100
Boileau, Lt-Col Francis, Bengal Artillery: commands artillery Mian Mir 29-32, approves Sarah's engagement 50; moves to Fort 58
Boileau, Lt Frank, 16th N.I.: friend of L 29, 36, 49, 50; at disarming 32; joins Punjab Bn. 47; takes Dogras to Haryana 48; at Hansi 71; wounded 73, 81; recovered 169
Boileau, Miss Grace: described 49; at disarming 32
Boileau, Mrs Sarah: at disarming 32; visited by L 36, 37, 45; family 44, 49; in barracks 48; approves Sarah's engagement 50
Boileau, Miss Sarah: *49*; meets L 49; at disarming 32; music with L 41, 45; described 50-1, 116; engaged 48-50; L leaves 52; letters to L 58, 86; likes Brownlow 109; wants L home 169; marriage 171; children 171-2; death 172
Bombay: *14*; Presidency of 16
Bourchier, Capt George, Bourchier's Light Battery: At Etawah 153
Brahmins: have to serve overseas 23; fear Christianity 23
Brasyer, Capt Jeremiah, Brasyer's Sikhs: at Capture 164-5
Bridge of Boats, Delhi: *54*; attacks on 55, 57, 63
Bridge of Boats, Lahore: *28*; L breaks up 42
Bridge of Boats, Lucknow: *124*; at Capture 163
Briscoe, Lt, 75th Foot: killed at Assault 95
Brook Green Militia: at Anarkullie 37
Brown Bess Rifle: 8th Regt use 60

Brownlow, 2nd-Lt Elliot, BE: *157*; at Addiscombe 157; family 157; friend of L 29, 157; character 75, 168; meets Lawrence 157; to Kashmir 29-30, 157; his letters 75, 116; has L's revolver 71; admires Sarah 116; at Capture 155, 156, 159, 164; death 166-9; last letters 170
Brownlow, Lt Henry, BE: at Siege 56-7; at Assault 94
Buckingham Palace: Mutiny levee 172; awards CB to L 173
'Buckingham Palace', Agra: Ladies' mess at, 112, 116
Bulandshahr: *98*; Column approaches 102, B of 103-5
Bungalows (D): *134*; at Capture 163
Burgess, Sgt F. BE: at Assault 93
Burma: L posted to 171
Burn Bastion: *88*; at Assault 95-6
Burn, Lt-Col Henry: at Assault 93
Bussaye: *54*; L visits bridge 62

Cactus Lane: *76*; at Assault 84
Calcutta: *14*; social style 15; HQ of EIC 16; letters via 150; troops from 155; L's gift to 172
Calcutta Gate: after Siege 101
Camels: *73*; use of 73; at Siege 83; at Relief 129; in Column 150
Campbell, General Sir Colin, C-in-C: *131*; background ix, 131; sent to India 74; gathers army 99-100, 125; Column waits for 126-9; at Relief 131-3; 135, 137, 140-1, 145; his plans after Relief 145, 155, 158; at Capture 159, 160, 167; criticized 131, 145, 147, 155, 158
Campbell, Brig-Gen George, 52nd Foot: at Assault 90
Canal St: *88*; at Assault, 92-3, 95
Canning, Lord, Governor-General: remote 39, promise to Wheeler 121
Cantonments, Delhi: *54, 66*; 56
Cantonments, Mian Mir: *28*; 26
Carmichael, Sgt A, BE: at Assault 93
Carnegie, 2nd-Lt Henry, BE: at Siege 56; at Capture 162
Cawnpore: *38, 110, 144*; fears for 47; massacre 59, 111, 120-3; Column at 120-6; Campbell's rescue plans

145-6; Bs of 146-8; troops gather before Capture 155-6, 158

Chambal R: *110*; Mhow Bde cross 113

Chamberlain, Brig-Gen Neville: with Movable Column 41; at Siege 42, 51

Champain, 2nd-Lt John Bateman BE: at Siege 56; at Assault 95

Champain's Battery: *66*; at Siege 68

Chandni Chowk: *88*; at Assault 90, 95-6; after Assault 100-1

Chattar Manzil: *124, 134, 154*; at Relief 136, 138, 141

Cheltenham College: L at 19

Chesney, Lt George, BE: at Siege 56, 68; at Assault 94

'China' Troops: diverted to India 37, 40; meet Column 126

Christianity: impact on British 20, 22-23, 26; on L 19; on Indians 23

Church, Cawnpore: *144*; target at B of Cawnpore 147

Church, Delhi: *76, 88*; at Assault 93

Church, Mian Mir: *28*; L uses as a watchtower 36-7

Chukkar Kothi: *154*; at Capture 161

Citadel: *see* Fort, Lahore

Clerke, Capt A.J., Royal Engineers: killed at Capture 166-7

Coehorn Mortars: at Siege 57

Cocks, Arthur, Sessions Judge Mainpuri: delays Column 119

Coghill, Capt Kendal, 1st Bengal Fusiliers: praises Lang 89

College: *88*; at Assault 94

Corbett, Mrs: her fears 30, 33

Corbett, Brig Stuart: commands troops at Mian Mir 29-35; pursues 26th NI 58; his resolution 75

Cotton, Col Henry, 67th NI: commands troops at Agra 115

Cracklow, Lt George, Bengal Artillery: with Columns 105, 151

Craigie, Lt Francis, Guides: at Siege 62

Crimean War: compared to Mutiny 149

Crow's Nest: *54, 66*; at Siege 57, 60, 70

Custom House: *76*; at Assault 86, 90

Dacres: *see* Wise

Dadri: *98*; column at 102

Dalhousie, Lord, former Governor-General: annexes Punjab 16, 24

Delhi: *14, 38, 54, 66, 76, 88, 98*; no news from 32, 36-7; mutiny at 34, 42; value of 39; Siege 42, 46, 51, 55-87; assault plan 77-8, 85; Assault 89-97; wounded sent there 106; success and losses at 117-8, 149, 155; L's feats at 172-3

Delhi Gate: *88*; at Assault 97

Derapur: *110*; Column at 152

Dilkusha Bridge: *134, 154*; at Relief 137, 142

Dilkusha House and Park: *124, 134, 154*; at Relief 136-8, 141-2, 145-6; at Capture 159-61

Dinajpur: *14*; Mutiny at 30

Diwan-i-Khas (King's Palace): looted 97

Doab: rumours of Wheeler's campaign in 46; Column enters 150

Dogras: go to Haryana 48

Drew, Capt Browning, 75th Foot: at Assault 95

Drunkenness: at Assault 94

East India Company or EIC (*see also* Indian Civil Service, Public Works Dept and Political Dept): nicknames 16; administration 16; officers' training 15-6

Elephants: *79*; in siege-train 79; at Siege 57-8; in Columns 112, 150; before Relief 129

Engineers' House: *54, 66*; 56

Entrenchment: *see* Fort, Cawnpore

Etawah: *110*; Column at 152-4

Etmadpur: *110*; column at 116

European Barracks: *see* Barracks

Examiner, The: reports on Mutiny 51

Excalibur (L's sword): sharpened 82; ineffective 92

Faqueer Takia picket: at Siege 59

Farrer, Rev Frederic, chaplain Mian Mir: reads service 35, 41

Fatehgarh: *38, 110*; sepoys hold 146, 152; Campbell consolidates at 155, leaves 158; L could be left at 155

Fateporah Masjid: at Assault 96

Firozabad: *110*; Column at 117

Firozpur: *38*; sepoys dispersed 32-3; to receive battalion from Karachi 37; sends siege-train 56

Flagstaff Tower: *54, 66*; at Siege 56-7, 60

Forbes, 2nd-Lt John, BE: at Siege 56; at Assault 94; with Column 116; at Relief 130, 141, at Capture 162

Fort, Agra: L visits 112, 116

Fort (Entrenchment), Cawnpore: *144*; British hold 147

Fort (Citadel), Lahore: *28*; arms to 30; ladies and treasure to 33, 35; Artillery to 58

Franks, Brig-Gen Edward: at Capture 160-1, 166

Fraser, Col Hugh, BE, Governor North-West Provinces: sends for Column 109; L meets 115

Friend of India: urges decimation 46; lauds B of Cawnpore 149

Freeling, Lt Walter, 46th NI (L's cousin): safe 46, 153; at Relief 135, 141-2, 146; at Capture 156, 159, 164, 166

Fulford, 2nd-Lt William, BE: at Siege 56

Fyzabad Rd: *154*; at Capture 161

Ganges R: *14, 38, 98, 110, 144*; camps near 146

Geneste, Lt Maximilian, BE: at Siege 56, 72; at Assault 95, 97

General's Mound: *54*; at Siege 61

Glover, Mrs: at Agra 112, 115

Gomati R: *38, 124, 134, 154*; at Relief 136-8, 141-2; at Capture 160-2

Goodwyn, Major Alfred, BE: at Relief 129, 137-8

Gooshahi Ganj: *110*; Column at 119-20

Gordon, Capt Charles, 75th Foot: at Agra 115

Gough, Capt Charles, Guides: at Siege 62, 72

Gough, Lt Hugh, Hodson's Horse: at Siege 61-2, 72; with Column 100, 104-7; at Relief 136

Gowan, Maj-Gen George, commanding Mian Mir: 29, 42, 51, 59

Grant, Brig-Gen J. Hope: commands Cavalry Bde at Delhi 62; commands Column 99, 118-20; commands Division at Relief 145, 149; commands Division at Capture 155

Grant, Lt-Gen. Sir Patrick, C-in-C Madras: admired by L 74

Greathed, Col Edward, 8th Foot: at Siege 83; commands Column 99-100, 105-111, 115; superseded 118; commands Bde at Cawnpore 147

Greathed, Lt William, BE: at Siege 56-7, 70, 83, 87; at Assault 90, 92, 94; at Capture 159, 167

Gulliver, Lt Henry, BE: at Mian Mir 29, 34, 37; at Siege 56, 61

Gurdaspur: *38*; 47

Gustavinski, Louis (Ski), BE: at Mian Mir 29, 34-7; takes Mazbis to Delhi 46-7; at Siege 60-1, 69; at Assault 94

Gwalior Contingent: [Gwalior *38*]; joins Mutiny 44; Delhi sepoys may have joined 95; target for Column 99; threat of 111, 133; Nana Sahib might join 126; at Cawnpore 145-9

Hansi: *38*; Frank Boileau at 71

Harrington, Lt Hastings, Bengal Artillery: stung by hornets 129

Harris, Mrs: letter from Lucknow 45

Harrow: Langs live at 16, 25; Langs go to Harrow School 19

Haryana: *38*; Frank Boileau at 48

Hathras: *98*; Column at 109

Havelock, Maj-Gen Sir Henry: beats Nana Sahib 59; marches north 108; relieves Lucknow 99-100, 125-6; at Relief 141; his death 146

Hay, Captain John, 60th NI: at Assault 90

Hazrat Ganj: *154*; at Capture 163-4

Health of troops: good 68, 109; cholera 78, 82; L unwell 81, cured with leeches 119-20; effects of Delhi campaign 132; nurses 116

Heathcote, Lt Alfred, 60th Rifles: at Siege 87

Herat (L's horse): vicious 26; at Delhi 70; saves L's life 114-5

Hildebrand, Lt Edward, Bengal Artillery: killed at Siege 83

Hindan R: *98*; Column at 100-1

Hindu Rao's House: *54, 66*; at Siege 56, 68-71

Hindus: fears of cartridges 20; hatred of Sikhs 24

Hisar: *38*; attacked 73

Hodson, Capt William: raises 'Plungers' 55; at Siege 71-2, 81; kills princes 100; dies 163

Hogge, Major, Commissary of Ordnance: at Siege 82

Holkar, Maharajah of Indore: 63

187